COLLECTIVE REFLECTIVE POWER:

A Memoir

SHAKIRA ZAYAH CH'I

COLLECTIVE REFLECTIVE POWER:
A Memoir

We are not our Mothers.
We are not our Fathers.
We must learn to choose our own path.
We are not inherently evil.
It's up to us, the now,
To make a difference for our future generations.
We must learn to walk our own spiritual path.

Taking this time to express myself takes a lot. I am one of those people who find it hard to accept a Band-Aid when it's obvious that I need it. Foolish pride some would say, but this idiosyncrasy I have is something that I'm working to change. So here I am talking to you. After meeting several people whose profession is social work. I let them know some things about my life. And they all came to the consensus that I should write a book. I was told by each, that they would love to read it. These very special people say I inspire them. Can you believe it? Me, inspire anyone! I get teary-eyed thinking of me being an inspiration. If you allow me to take you on my journey and take a peep into my world, then hopefully, you too will be inspired.

300 fourscore years ago-okay just joking! I'm not trying to digress, it's just that I believe in life sometimes, we must laugh to keep from crying. Kind of like making lemonade out of lemons. That's my mantra that has kept me alive.

So anyways my mother was raised in a large military family. My maternal grand-father was a Navy man, so he wasn't home much. My maternal grandmother held jobs as a secretary, Sheriff and social worker. Trying to help support eight children I could imagine was not an easy task. My mother was actually born a twin. Her twin brother whose name was Tracy, sadly passed away when he was just six months old. He lost his battle with pneumonia. I have cried for my uncle whom I never knew so many times. I wish that he was here and I hope that he can see me. I wish to let him know that I love him. Out of my extended maternal family, my mom was the different one. Petite, light-skinned, freckles and small pointy nose. Which is a contrast to my aunts and uncles. My mom has said that she takes after her maternal grandmother. My maternal great-grandmother was herself very pale. She could've very well had passed for white. It was believed that great-grandmother was mixed with native blood. I have since found out through DNA test that we have no native blood. One of my uncles hinted that my mother is a product of rape by a white man against my grandmother. Whatever the case may be, my mom was different. Smart, artsy, quirky. She was the only one out of her family to attend college. She would have graduated I'm told, had she not gotten pregnant with me. Despite her seem-ing appearance of intellectual gifts, she was nicknamed Dodi by her mother and siblings(their alternative to dodo). Could you imagine on record as being a intelligent person but your family calls you dumb basically. What an irony. So my parents were high school sweethearts. My father grew up on the opposite side of the tracks. My paternal grandfather was a carpenter and my paternal grandmother was a homemaker. God bless their souls. My dad had a head on his shoulders. Tall, thin, dark and I guess handsome. My mom would not let me forget that he grew up poor, that he grew up in the projects. She acted as if he were a different species or something. The way the story goes. Boy sees girl, girl doesn't like the boy, but the boy is very persistent. Girl begins to like boy, girl loses virginity to boy. They move in together, get married, have a child yada yada yada. You know how the story goes. Well in this one everything kind of falls apart after the child, me. I don't remember much of my parents being together as I was only about four when my dad split. I guess I was destined to be a fighter. From what my mom told me, my dad was a fast guy. He himself had his first child when he was only 14. "You know how those project people are" is what my mom would say. But knowing that made her yearn for a child with him that much more. My dad was one of those people always searching, for what I don't know. My mother is one of those people who is content no matter what. But through her pseudo-contentment she'd loved to drink liquor. My dad was out and about trying to find something. Somewhere to be long or maybe the answer to his burning question about life. He was an avid reader and loved music. Bob Marley, Peter Tosh pretty much anyone who was Afrocentric or had something to say, he listened. This led to my mother being lonely most of the time from what I was told. My mother was quite the opposite. She didn't agree with Afrocentrism and she didn't believe that racism still existed in America. But despite her outwardly pacification, something was stirring in her spirit that caused her to drink heavy. From what I'm told, my mother wanted a baby desperately. I guess anything or anyone to keep her for being lonely or to keep my dad home. She said that a few months prior to becoming pregnant with me, she had a miscarriage. She admitted that she was drinking like a sailor around that time but doesn't attribute it to her miscarriage. According to her that put her into a deeper depression. She drank vodka and prayed, prayed and drank vodka. Lo and behold she became pregnant with me. She said that I was the answer to her prayers. She thought that she couldn't have children, that maybe she had some kind of reproductive fault. Well, I stayed in the oven even though I must have been tipsy a lot. Mother drank quite less when she found out that she was pregnant this time, good for her! I tell you, me and my fighting spirit. I probably would have aborted myself if I knew all the hell I was about to face, but that wasn't written. June 7th, 1978 was my turn to come into this dimension, I was born by C-section. The doctors placed my mom in the hospital two months before I was born because she developed gestational diabetes. Could it be the liquor that added to the disease, maybe? Regardless of her illness, I was born healthy and strong weighing 8 pounds 1 ounce.

By my mom being so artistically inclined, she had knitted some hats and booties for me. I saw them in her closet when I got older and was shocked that she saved them for all those years. I was touched to know that she made those articles by hand for me. However I was not touched by the putrid 70s colors. You know the vomit green, burnt orange and rusty brown. Knitted together to make one color scheme. But hey it's the thought that counts right?

I have a few fond memories. I recall the days when I was a very young child my mother would hug me and my father would pick me up and squeeze me tight.Growing up I would see my mom's art supplies all around the house. She did art as a hobby by this time because she never went back to VCU to get her degree. By this time my dad had decided to go to college. And the way my mom tells the story "He could have never got into VCU (a prominent college in Virginia) if it wasn't for me". My dad's major, criminal justice. Even though my father wasn't around much when he was home I felt that he loved me, I was a daddy's girl. Not that I didn't love my mom, it's just that she wasn't that emotional. She provided well for me and brought me the nicest clothes, newest toys, taught me my ABCs, cooked good meals which was evident in my stature. I had always been a chubby child.

We just didn't connect for some reason. It was like she didn't know how to appeal to a child. Through it all, I loved my mom with every drop of blood in my body. It was a gradual separation for my parents. Dad would stay gone for one day, and then two days come back home and do it all over again. I recall that dreadful morning my mother let my father in, she was getting ready for work. When I heard my dad come home I got out of bed and ran to see him. He picked me up, hugged and kissed me and offered to make me breakfast. Between you and I my dad wasn't a great cook! He made the hardest scrambled eggs. But they were good to me once he put ketchup on them. My dad and I sat together in front of the TV watching Rev. Ike. Eating our hard cooked scrambled eggs with ketchup. I was the happiest little girl at that moment.

I should have known that, this feeling wouldn't last long. That was the last time my dad came home. It seems this was a prelude to my life's song. For me, great joy before immense pain. After father left, my mother was hired to work at Richmond Times dispatch then called Richmond news leader (a local newspaper company). My maternal grandfather worked there driving trucks to various locations to distribute the newspapers. So long story short my grand-dad got my mom a job working graveyard shift in the printing department. Physical work but it paid pretty good for the early 80s. With my dad gone it meant that I spent more time with my maternal grandma. She would watch me while my mom worked nights. Now my maternal grandparents also had a very tumultuous marriage. By this time, they themselves had been separated for some years. When my mother was little, from what I was told, witnessed very violent and bloody arguments between my maternal grandparents. My grandmother had her own issues with alcohol. She didn't seem to like me very much. She was a heavy drinker and when she drank, she didn't say the nicest things to me. Suddenly I become the target of her verbal assault. One of my cousins, who was at my grandma's house as often as I was, was three years older than me. This cousin(named Chris) was an only child, which I believe led to him to being a mischievous, spoiled brat. He did so many devious things, too many to keep track of. I would tell my grandma that he was the guilty party, but no matter what, she blamed me. Like I was a devil child, but as I got older, I started to realize that she may have had some unresolved negative feelings towards my mother. Maybe because her son (my mom's twin brother) died, and she was reminded of that pain when she looked at my mother or her offspring. Maybe my grandmother was raped which produced my mom, or maybe my mom was indeed a devil child and my grandma saw me as guilty by association. I believe the latter but whenever the case may be, my grandma's words hurt me deeply. But for as many times she hurt me there were times when I believed she cared. I remember when I turned five and my mother being single couldn't afford to throw me a party. She had to pay her own rent, utilities, car note, food etc. All living expenses without the help of my father. He never paid one dime towards my support,but that's another issue.Anyway my mother really wanted to have a birthday party for me. So she went to my grandmother and asked her to finance and host my first and sadly my last birthday party. My mother expressed to me that my grandmother was obliged to do so.I invited every child from the neighborhood,some who I didn't even play with.But in my book that was not important.What good was having a party if I didn't share my special day with other children?Although some were actually teens, it made no difference to me.

I recall one time when I was following behind my older cousin,Chris, who went to play drive in my mom's Ford Pinto. It so happened that my grandmother lived on a hill. So I was in the passenger seat and my cousin was in the driver seat. He simulated driving as I eagerly sat beside him. Somehow he hit the gearshift, which caused the car to move downhill. Before I knew it, my cousin opened the driver side door and leapt out of the car. I made a desperate attempt to do the same. But somehow I fell and got stuck under the carriage. I was crying out for dear life and my cousin ran to get help. Several men from the neighborhood came to my aid. My grandmother and mother came outside. Frantically they all attempted to pull me from under the car but to no avail. My cousin was standing back watching. I have always wondered did he try to intentionally lure me to my early demise with all the crazy stunts he pulled?

Out of nowhere came Peewee, a neighborhood boy older than me that I never played with,but I invited to my party. I saw this black hand reaching out to me, I looked into his light hazel eyes and he calmly said "Grab my hand". To everyone's amazement he pulled me from under that wretched car.I think by him being able to calm me down is what made him successful. My mom rushed to pick me up.My legs were bleeding and she feared the worst.

As all of this is transpiring, the Pinto was rolling downhill. As God had it written, the wheel was turned all the way left. Which caused my mom's car to roll into an empty field by grandma's house. Had it rolled straight downhill, it would have caused major destruction. Because there was a busy street at the foot of the hill.

My mom and grandma rushed me to the ER at MCV, one of the best local hospitals. Once there, the doctors gave me x-rays. Fearing that the car may have broken pelvic or leg bones, but by God's grace no bones were broken! In the course of me being stuck, my thighs rubbed together and the friction caused some bleeding. Of course once better, my grandmother blamed me for following behind my cousin. That was a hard lesson learned, but I learned not to follow my crazy cousin. I could have died or been paralyzed.

At that time I had only one girl cousin, Neh Neh. We got along good when we saw each other, which was rare. One day in particular I can't forget. It was Neh Neh, my four boy cousins from a different aunt. Their names Junie, Tony (R. I. P.), Mike, Nick and myself. My cousin Chris was away staying with his father. We all had been playing throughout the day as we normally did together. Night fell and grandma sent us to bed upstairs. Neh Neh and I took our aunts' room and the boys took our uncles' room. Neither of them were at home at that time. As I'm lying down asleep, I was awakened by my oldest cousins dragging me into my uncles room. They pinned me down on my uncles bed and tried to force my cousin Nick (who is four months younger than me) to rape me. I was crying, kicking and screaming with all my might. And they still continued to try and coerce Nick to rape me. Apparently they thought that he was gay. So in their twisted logic, raping and committing incest was suppose to make a man out of him. Whilst this was happening my girl cousin was standing there with her mouth wide open saying "Aww"! She didn't go to get grandma but just stood there watching as I kicked and screamed for help.

After the older boys saw that I would continue fighting and that Nick wasn't with the program they let up. I ran downstairs for dear life. "Grandma, grandma" I said "they tried to rape me, they held me down" Her retort as she was sitting on her daybed, drinking a screwdriver (her favorite drink of orange juice and vodka) puffing on a kool menthol cigarette. "Girl didn't nobody try nothing with you now take your butt to bed." Terrified to go back upstairs, I went into the front room and napped on the sofa. That itself for me was a great feat, as I was afraid of the dark. Being a Gemini child, my vivid imagination ran away at times, especially after seeing something scary. I was just crazy about Michael Jackson in the early 80s but after thriller I was utterly put off by him. He completely horrified me by turning into that zombie. It took years for me to trust watching any of his videos again. The following morning when my mom returned from work, she brought my school clothes and gave me a bath. So as she's bathing me I was in a quasi-catatonic state. In utter shock at what had transpired the night before.Neh Neh burst into the bathroom saying "Aunt Dodi,Kira got raped" My mother calmly and softly asked me "Is that true"? I simply shook my head. I didn't coo one word. From that point on I had my reservations about Neh Neh. So quick to report that she believed I was raped, but made no effort to assist me that night.

My mother was an very attractive young woman. So this meant finding another man was no problem for her. In my eyes there was only one man for her, my dad. But that was not the way the cookie crumbled. There were more boyfriends that I care to count. And all of them with the exception of one had this in common, they didn't seem to truly care for or love my mom, needless to say me. It was as if she was their good time girl. They could come to her apartment and eat, drink, smoke weed and you know what else. Around this time I started to view my mom as an,I hate to say it,but a whore. Simple and plain.I didn't understand the life of a single woman and still don't for that matter. Although there was this one nice guy, I'll call him O. He was a little younger than my mother. Newly recruited to the Marines, originally from Georgia, he was moving back. There in Georgia he had planned to finish his career, acquire a nice home on the barracks and get married. He wanted my mom to be his wife and me his daughter. He was the only man of all the scum she dated, who treated her the way I thought she should be treated. He seemed to really love her. You know the one in a million man who buys you flowers just because.

Who doesn't forget your anniversary. Who loves you through thick and thin, the extra 20 pounds and all. But no she didn't want that.

It was Christmas eve 1983, he knocked on the door bearing gifts for me and mom. He wanted to come inside but she wouldn't allow it. His watery eyes looked deep into my mother's. I was standing right there beside her observing everything. "Would you come with me please, I already have an home there and we can get married." "No" she responded "I'm happy here and I'm not ready to get married". "Are you sure"? One blink away from a tear rolling down his face. "Yes" my mom retorted. He turned and walked away like a defeated soldier. He didn't know it but I was rooting for him. I wanted to cry for him. For a while after that night I wondered what became of him. Was he successful in his career? Did he find another woman whom he loved equally? As I got older I wondered if the pain my mom caused hardened him towards women?

Mom had this one boyfriend who I as a child called grease monkey, he was a mechanic and coupled with his looks or lack thereof, that was a fitting title! Anyways when he was around, my mom showed me no attention. Nada! It turns out that he was separated from his wife yet they still lived together. Separate bedrooms supposedly. Once, this grease monkey, let me be nice I'll call him Tee.

Tee brought his son over my mom's place with him. My mother had the audacity to let his son play with my space shuttle riding toy. Oh my God, I was livid. I already didn't like him (he was such a mooch eating my mom's food, watching her TV, etc.) so how was I to like his son? I didn't care that he was a little younger than me. And to make matters worse Tee never even acknowledged me. His jerry curl completely disgusted me.

Not long after Tee, my mother met someone who would forever change my life. With this person, I looked unadulterated evil directly into the eyes. Strange thing is, I was initially entranced by this entity that I did not understand. Who is he? Where did he come from? What is he? When I first saw him, I saw pain, I saw loneliness, I saw a person who never seemed to belong.

I recognized this because those were my very own feelings. I never felt I belonged, never felt a part of the pack. It seemed to me that I was always on the outside looking in. A loner at such an early age, but it is what it is.I was curious about him but I didn't like him, I did not trust him. Was he like the rest? Here to use my mom and leave. I watched him like an mongoose watches a snake, cautious and observing. He was younger than my mom, only 21 and my mother was 29. No one in my mom's family liked him. Was it his age, was it how he looked (some people thought he was Hispanic, Greek, Italian, Indian, you name it. No one could pan his race) or was it that he was trouble? Word on the street at that time was that he was a crazy motherfucker. Running with gangs, robbing people and who knows what else. I'm certain that these allegations were true considering that his best friend,his right-hand man. Is now on death row in North Carolina for double murder. And those are the ones (according to the street) he got caught for! Rumor has it that his friend bodied (murdered) at least 15 people.

My mom's new boyfriend's name was Greg. Reddish-brown complexion, average height, average build, small red piercing eyes. What stood out the most about him, was his long black wavy hair. It garnered attention everywhere he went. And you know how us black folk love some shiny wavy hair (we call it good hair) as if there is a such thing as bad hair! Go figure, us and our peculiar sayings. So anyway my mother had this thing like she believed he was a catch. He was younger than her and exotic looking. That's about all he had going for him. No education, no job, no money. But he always dressed good though. With clothes he stole from various department stores.

It was hard at first to let my guard down, but him being a devil appealed to my feelings of alienation. He insisted that I accompany them on their quasi-dates. I was invited to go with them to the movies, the park, picnics, you name it. He didn't want me excluded from any aspect of their social life. By him including me in their social life, I started to let my guard down. I saw him in a different light. Maybe he could be my new father, which I desperately wanted. I missed and loved my daddy so much. And mom wasn't letting me visit my dad or my extended paternal family for that matter. Raymond, my father, did make efforts to visit me on holidays, my birthdays included. He brought me very nice gifts at these times but Janet(my mother) would take them before I could get a good look and give them to her nieces and nephews. If they weren't around she'd throw them away. It's like I was a pawn in her twisted revenge plot to hurt Raymond in any way she could. She tried with all her might to make me think lowly of him. Calling him and his family ignorant project ghetto trash. In my younger years, when I had the gift of staying with grandma Rebecca and grandpa James, I never saw this. I only saw kind ,humble people whom I knew without a shadow of doubt loved me. Never a harsh word towards me. I didn't even hear them use profanity. They showed the utmost care, respect and concern for me.

So being that I was forbidden to have contact with my biological father, the second best I thought was Greg. Out of my sharing, this I found the most difficult to share. As this was the beginning of a saga that would take 28 years to escape.

In the beginning all that surrounded him was negativity. No one seemed to like him, he was estranged from his father, at odds with his grandmother. Disgruntled with aunts and uncles. My mother's family absolutely despised him. He explained to me, that he was treated this way because most people including his family, were downright jealous of him.

He didn't really know his mother. As he was the product of an interracial relationship. From what he expressed to me. His mother, a girl at the time of his birth, was an 14-year-old runaway. Of Italian, German and Vietnamese descent. Her father, Greg's maternal grandfather, was Italian with some Vietnamese ancestry. He was a peasant who married a wealthy German woman, they subsequently had three children. It's unclear how, but his grandfather met an early death. His maternal grandmother emigrated to America. Once here, she remarried the founder of RCA. Then an up-and-coming company headquartered in Camden, New Jersey. Why did his mother choose to run away, when she came from such a wealthy background? I have yearned to ask her directly. But unfortunately she passed away before I could meet her. Before she could unite with her oldest son and meet any of her grandchildren fathered by him.

Because of these facts, because of him not having a bountiful relationship with his mother or father. I almost instantly felt pity for him, I've always been one who possess a nurturing spirit. I'm a person who tries not to step on ants, who prays for the safety of a squirrel attempting to cross the street, who truly weeps for the even less fortunate peoples of third world countries. So me knowing this, was the beginning of everything being put into place by him. The first stages of his brainwashing tactics.

Wary of him in the beginning, I eventually warmed up to him.

He would buy me these gigantic handmade lollipops and mind you, I loved sweets. He would let me stay up late and took time to talk to me. I slowly started to see him in a positive light.

So the more time I spent with him, my mom felt comfortable to let him watch me while she worked. So I saw my grandparents and extended family less and less.Until eventually my mother and I stopped seeing them completely. But in my mind it was all good. Being that he by this time had gained my trust.

I told him about the ill-treatment I received sometimes at my grandmother's house. In my mind at that time he was my Savior. He had also convinced my mom that her siblings were all out to use, degrade and downright hated her. So with these antics he managed to isolate us. Excommunicate us from any family or outside influence. As my mother wasn't social with anyone but her family and neither was I. Thinking back I recall,that it seemed like the perfect small family at first. But he started to become more controlling and aggressive towards my mother. I recall the first time I witnessed him punching her, I immediately ran up to him while shouting "Don't hit my mama". Pulling on his legs, hitting him with my small fist, as I was only about six at the time. He quickly admonished me, "If you don't stop hitting me and go in your room, I'm going to beat your ass" When he said this I reluctantly did as he asked. I was petrified of the belt or any kind of corporal punishment. Because my mother had never spanked me. So that alone instilled fear in me. So vividly I think back to all the times I saw my mom with black eyes, at times both eyes were black. As well as bruises over her body. Sitting in the corner crying, I would walk to her (of course when he was in another room) and ask her if she was okay. She would say "Momma is okay, give me a hug" She'd muster a smile, through her stricken face and tears. And I would hug her crying myself, feeling immense sorrow. I recall once, (I believe not long after my first brother was born) Greg caused my mother to be hospitalized. She had to stay for several days. He beat her so badly that both her eyes and ears were swollen. He pounded her in the head and ears. The doctors feared that she would become deaf.And they begged her at the time to tell who did that to her but her loyalty to him wouldn't allow it. That's how much damage he did to her. She can still hear, but her ears have been permanently disfigured. To this day when I look at her ears, I think about those days and wonder how does she still love him?

So with Greg around things started to change drastically. No more PTA meetings. No more paying bills on time. No more family visits. No more of me going to school everyday. My grades had started to drop by this time. I was in second grade and up until that point I made straight A's in every subject. So by all means, he let us know who was in control! We eventually were evicted from our apartment in Henrico County .The site where we once lived, is now the Richmond International Raceway! A lot of big-time racecar drivers have raced there including Dale Earnhardt!

My baby brother was now about an year old. Greg and my mother had quit their jobs at the newspaper company. My mother had helped Greg obtain a job there. But there was some rift about her sleeping with guys from the job. Greg claimed that just about every guy in that department had slept with my mother. So my mom attempted to counter act the accusations by confronting one of the guys spreading these rumors. She reportedly grabbed this guy by the throat and threatened him. This happened in front of every employee in that area. So someone told corporate. Corporate in response to the incident attempted to get my mother to admit her wrong. By insisting that she sign a written confession. Afterwards she unknowingly would have been arrested for assault, which was a felony.

Because Greg was present in the meeting with her, he snatched the pen from her and spoke on her behalf. He let them know that she wasn't going to sign this paper and that they both quit. So as you may have figured the majority of their arguments were fueled by his belief that she was cheating. He would often come to me with tears in his eyes saying "I know you think I'm a bad person, I know you hate me. You see how me and your mom fight. That's because she's always fucking around and that hurts" "I love her so much, I've never had anyone to love me. My mama left me when I was a baby, my dad never loved me, he treated me so cold. He kicked me out when I was 16." "So I had to rough it on the street. I had to join up with the gang to survive because people were always jealous of me, trying to hurt me". "One day, Kira (my nickname) you'll see it's not me" "When you love someone sometimes you do the wrong things for the right reason". By this time his projected pain caused me to cry. I would tell him that I forgave him, how much I loved him and that I understood. Crazy right?

He is the most manipulative person I have ever encountered and hopefully ever will. So when he said my mom was cheating after a while I started to believe it. Reflecting on the days of me seeing her with many boyfriends. By me being afraid of the dark I would often have nightmares and run into her room to find solace, only to find her in the bed with some guy on top of her.

So that caused me to have a negative opinion of my mother. I began to withdraw from her. He then in return became my best friend.

When ever I had a problem, I went to him. Whenever I had a question, I went to him. And there were many as I was an curious child. I slowly started to lose respect for my mom. Not in a way where I verbally disrespected her. I continued to be respectful and obedient, but I guess I started to think that she wasn't the wisest person after all. With him constantly degrading her in my presence, how could I think otherwise.

So we had moved from our old apartment and were now living in Nottingham Apartments (a shabby apartment complex just a couple of miles from our old place). It was a one-bedroom apartment. On the lower level there was a living room, a walk in closet, the kitchen, the front door as well as a backdoor. Upstairs there was the bedroom and bathroom. My mother has stopped working completely, Greg then went to work, as the sole bread-winner. He got a pretty decent job working at Hostess bakery. He was making reportedly $11 an hour, which was very good money in 1987. So with his newly found wealth, he brought the largest TV, a new sofa bed that cost $1000. Upstairs, my bed was secondhand. Besides those things there wasn't much more furniture.

In school things started to get really tough for me, not academically but socially. When Greg would pick me up from school, I would happily introduce him to my classmates as my dad. The next day they would treat me differently. I would thereafter be shunned. Being a person of color, of African stock, in our American culture. We generally don't embrace anything or anyone that's different. Especially when you're black, but a different kind of black. So this pushed me to be somewhat of a loner in school. I had only one friend when I attended Ginter Park school. Melissa, a Caucasian girl, sadly wasn't in my class so we could only play at recess. She never treated me different, she never cared about how I look or who my dad was or what I was mixed with.

I often think of her and wonder how she's doing. I wonder would we remember each other if we saw each other. We were only about seven or eight so that was a pretty long time ago.

And home things were hectic. It was now my job to do all household chores. When I say all, I mean all. Dumping the trash, cleaning the kitchen from top to bottom, scrubbing the floors, cleaning my room, then the front room (their bedroom), cleaning the bathroom several times a day. Greg loved to take showers often. At this apartment we had poor plumbing. When he decided to take a bath I had to run his water, gather all of his grooming supplies, deodorant and clean underwear. After bathing I had to dump his dirty water out of the tub with a bucket into the toilet. Because something was wrong with the drain and he never bothered to buy drain clog remover or call maintenance. I mean I was his virtual slave. And to top that off, I was required to run to the corner store several times a day, do laundry all while expected to do my homework and perform well in school. I better had not overslept in the morning before school or else my mother would violently wake me up! Had I forgot to do or finish a chore that was grounds for a spanking. Usually carried out by Greg with an extension cord. My mother never intervened out of fear of him or her disdain for me, I'm not sure.

Some of the past memories I shared with you are very difficult to express, but this is very painful to recall. I have spent so many years blocking this memory. It's like I put it away in a time capsule to never be opened in this lifetime. But now is the time! I must tell the world, for I have not any shame. And I'm tired of holding the impious secrets of an nefarious being that I once called "Daddy".

The day of the week, the exact date or time when this horrible event occurred, I can't tell you. Because honestly I don't remember.

But I do recall that it was some time in early June. As I previously mentioned, he at that time had a well-paying job. My birthday June 7, the year 1987 was just around the corner.

This year he had promised to buy something nice for my birthday. I had lost all of my toys in the process of being evicted from our last apartment. He always confused me like that. One moment he's beating me for not taking out the trash (which I always thought was more of a job for men), the next minute he's promising to buy me toys, new clothes, etc.

Then the next minute he's calmly answering any questions I may have and praising me for being a smart child. Followed by screams of vulgar, degrading name-calling.

Like any eight-year old I was filled with anticipation. Wondering what I might receive for my ninth birthday just days away. Finally the big day arrived and in the mid-afternoon he gave me my gifts.

A connect four game, Cabbage Patch a.m. radio, three short sets (purple, green and blue my favorite colors) a pair of jelly sandals (called jellies because they were soft and clear) and ink pen set that contained a pearl necklace and bracelet (my birthstone) All of these items purchased from Thalheimers. A fancy upscale department store similar to Macy's, but has been out of business for many years now. In Richmond if you shopped out of Thalheimers you were doing it big. What he did to me was something I could never foresee. Totally out of nowhere like the summer rain. You know the ones when its hot and sunny one moment then next it turns dark and gloomy with sheets of rain. Like any given day nothing stood out. You know, I had just turned nine, I was really happy about my gifts. Elated to be on summer break. Greg frequently shopped and sold items at local flea markets. It was a way to make a little extra income. So on one of those flea market sprees (I call it) he purchased this belt that he named Freddy, after Nightmare On Elm Street. I was petrified of Freddy, the demon from the movie and Freddie, the belt. This belt was huge. About 7 inches wide and may be 3 inches thick. So one day I forgot to do a chore, for the life of me I couldn't tell you what chore exactly. He came upstairs to my room and told me that he was going to spank me. Not only spank me, but spank me with Freddy. I began to cry, fearful and begging that he not spank me. I was completely horrified. So he left out of the bedroom, went into the bathroom which was next to my bedroom and brought back a small jar of vaseline. He said "I know something you can do so I won't spank you" I cried to him "Please don't spank me, I'm sorry". He replied "Lie down, lie down on the bed on your stomach". Reluctantly I complied crying all the while. He calmly pulled up my t-shirt, pulled down my shorts and underwear. I'm was lying down crying and confused. Not understanding what he was doing or why. Next he put a large glob of vaseline on my anus. Next thing I know he is on top of me with his penis inserted in my rear. I cried louder, he told me to "shut up before I beat you"

He then directed me to put my head in the pillow. So I buried my head into the pillow crying from the physical pain. I could not comprehend what was happening. Why did he do this to me? He never showed any sexual longings towards me before. He was my father figure, albeit a cruel one at times, but nonetheless he was my father and I his child.

That first ordeal lasted about five minutes, but to me it felt like eternity. After he finished, he whispered to me that "You better not tell your mom" and that I had to " get yourself together, stop crying and don't act different around me". I stayed in my room the rest of the day. In complete shock, I felt betrayed, dirty, violated and alone. I felt as if God had cursed me. Was I only here for everyone near and dear to inflict pain on me? Metaphorically, I felt like an outdoor rug, here for everyone's use. After that day I don't know what happened to me mentally. Because every day seemed like a blur. Like I wasn't there. Sadly that wasn't the only time he sodomized me. This heinous act carried on at least twice a week for the next few years. He took this long before he decided to rape me vaginally. Whenever he wanted to rape me, he would fabricate some chore he said I didn't do. He would tell my mom that he was going to my room spank me. In reality he was coming to get his perverted fix.

After a while the physical pain dulled. I got used to it, but I never got used to feeling dirty.

For so many years I wanted to tell my mother what he was doing to me, but I was afraid. Afraid of what he'd do to me and what he'd do to her. He had this uncanny ability to make you believe what he wanted you to believe. He would often tell me that my mom would never leave him and that she would take his side. He was right as I found out when I told her two years later. Being in that situation caused me to feel even more like an outsider, no matter where I went. The store, school or church. I felt as if I were the living dead. I periodically went to church with his grandmother. She became my only grandmotherly influence. A devout yet hypocritical Pentecostal, so I had no trust there. Once he started raping me, he and my mother fought less. I still had chores to do but now I got an occasional day off. You know he was a nice guy like that, go figure! We moved from this apartment because the whole front room ceiling had caved in. The bathroom was situated directly above the front room. So those plumbing problems finally gave way. All the better for me because I was tired of dumping his dirty bathwater by hand into the toilet. We then moved into the West end of Richmond, which was somewhat of a yuppie, liberal area. Or shall I say Southern liberal. By this time my mother was pregnant with my second brother. He had lost his job and my mom was then the breadwinner. She went to work where he once worked. With so much time on his hands he began to teach me things that certainly no parent should teach their child. I recall him teaching me how to steal, teaching me how to shoot guns all while teaching me about the Bible.

Growing up, I always had an affinity for Christ. Sometimes I would cry myself to sleep asking God why did he allow them to murder him on the cross. For some reason I felt that God was my only friend in this life. So when he began telling me that he was a prophet sent here by God to unite all people I believed him. He from the very start shaped my perceptions. He came into my life in my most formative years. And I had no one else to tell me otherwise. I mean why else would God allow him to appeal to everyone? I thought to myself, I now realize that he planted those notions. No one could pinpoint his race. Latinos thought he was Latino, Asians thought he was Asian, Native Americans thought he was native American, Indians thought he was Indian, whites thought he was half white. I'm not quite sure what black people thought he was but they were seemingly mystified just the same.

That was the only plausible explanation I could think of. And who was I to rob humanity of the potential for racial and religious peace. Harmony on earth, where everyone loves one another. No conflict, no wars, no oppression. He was here to do that then more power to him. Yes, I know what he did to me was atrocious. But according to him there was nothing wrong with what he did to me. "You aren't my biological daughter, back in the old days men were permitted to marry girls your age and plus no one is perfect". "Noah was a drunkard but look how he saved the world". You must be thinking how can she be so gullible, but all I had to believe was what he told me. He had isolated me since I was a very young child. He actually made me believe that he was only person I could trust.

Not to mention he would frequently ask me "You don't want me to die do you"? "No" I quickly responded. "Okay well thats what would happen to me if you told anybody and got me locked up".

So yes, I grew up in a state of utter confusion. One part of me hated each fiber of his being, which I believe is a justified emotion. Another part of me thought that he was an modern day Messiah. Possibly an angel who made some awful mistakes but only because "he loves me so much".

A short time after leaving Nottingham Apartments, they entertained the idea of our then small family relocating to Florida. I don't know what was going through his mind exactly. But he said often how he was tired of Virginia. Tired of his extended family not helping him in any way. So we packed up our few belongings into his prized 1985 gold Caprice classic and headed to Florida. Jacksonville of all places. I recall it was a 13 Hour drive from Virginia. When we reached North Carolina, a lady who was obviously under the influence of alcohol, rammed right into the right passenger-side. She caused major damage to the car. Afterwards he and she pulled over. She was yelling that it was his fault and that he had to call the police. She was wobbling and disheveled. So he talked to her for a while and whatever he was saying didn't calm her down. The next thing I know he hopped back into the car and drove off. I asked "Why, why did you drive off daddy"? "Because" he replied "I don't have insurance and my license is suspended" I then said "But she was wrong, she drove into your car". "I know but that doesn't matter because I'm not supposed to be driving". So from that point on we didn't stop until we reached Florida.

When we first reached the toll bridge to get into Florida, I was very excited. I saw the palm trees, felt the warm air, even felt my ears pop. "My ears feel funny" I told him. "That's because it's a change in the atmosphere, we're so many feet below sea level" he said. "Really", I replied.

I had envisioned Florida being this place of unlimited riches and enchanting beauty. But instead all I saw was poverty, crime and classism. I mean I never had witnessed poor whites before. I'm sure Virginia has its share of poor whites but I wasn't exposed to that prior to us living in Florida. I remember so clearly on one side of Jacksonville was where all the poor people lived, black, white and Latino. Here, people were robbed in broad daylight, openly robbed grocery stores for food, sold blood to get their next meal.

We stayed in the Salvation Army homeless shelter while there. And in this shelter each family had one private room to share. (Unlike some shelters where it was dormitory or ward style). I had never witnessed such economic despair amongst Americans of European descent.

The city I'm from, I had always perceived the economic divide to be purely racial. That was actually an enlightening experience for me. I saw that this dreadful existence was not solely resigned for blacks and immigrants. Our neighbors in the room next to us was an poor white family, that consisted of husband, wife and two children. We became friendly with each other, and through occasional conversation, it was revealed that to make ends meet the husband would have his wife sell her blood. Which only brought in about $25-$30 each time. He would drive her to various locations throughout Jacksonville because a person was only allowed to sell so much blood a week. I felt sorry for her. It was obviously taking a toll on her health. It seemed that she grew weaker and weaker by the day. Faint and frail, he had no shame in the treatment of her. And to make matters worse he didn't sell his blood. He used her, his wife and mother of his children as if she were his tool. Selling her life force for a few dollars, hot dog and a soda. As I grew older and wiser, I thought about her and guessed that he must have been a junkie, though I didn't witness him use drugs.

At that time I never knew that I myself would be in a similar situation.I thought I could escape my hell peacefully in the near future.When I was an adult of course,I thought the longest I would have to deal with this torment would be until I was 18.Like 18 was a magic number.But I now realize that adulthood is not defined by age but mental and economic power.And you can't leave hell in a peaceful manner. So after being homeless in Florida for a few weeks, my parents (I so blindly called them at that time) decided that wasn't their scene. So they decided or shall I say he decided that it was time to go. My mother didn't have much rank in decision-making. So we packed up our belongings, what few we had, in to that wretched chitty chitty bang bang and headed back to Virginia. By the time we had reached North Carolina, Greg had been pulled over by a state trooper. After a license check, the police found that he was driving on a suspended license. So the officer placed Greg under arrest,towed his beloved Caprice classic and gave my mom and I a ride back to the local police station that tripled as a local jail and court.

It so happened that the town judge lived in a house behind the station/jail. This is one of those situations where at the time was pretty scary but now I can look back on it and actually laugh! Being a Virginia native I had never realized what a deep southern accent must sound like. But boy did I when I heard the local sheriff speak. He had the deepest southern drawl I had heard personally to this day. They had quite a few men locked up for various reasons. Some were quiet while this one guy in particular kept complaining how he wanted to be released. I guess for him it was partly due to it being a culture shock, probably because of his charges (cannot recall exactly what they were) but he had to stand before the local judge. Court didn't open until the next business day and it was the weekend. So the sheriff, a stocky black guy with shortcut hair and a mustache verbally snapped on him. The sheriff said in a deep may I reiterate deep southern drawl "Look be quiet now,win you bak dere you jus bak dere" Needless to say the inmate got quiet for a little while. The sheriff was courteous to my mother and I. He even offered us one of the bag lunches that was provided for the inmates. It consisted of on that day a bologna sandwich with a slice of bologna about 2 inches thick, American cheese about 1 inch thick, a small bag of chips and a little Debbie oatmeal cream pie. He even offered my mother a cell to lie down in because she was pregnant with my baby brother at the time. She declined, her and I sat in the small area that had four chairs right in front of the front desk. We stayed there all that day into the next morning. By this time Greg had received the money transfer that his grandmother had sent to pay his fines. So we could at least make it back to Virginia. After paying his fines, the police admonished him that he could be stopped again in another state. They made him aware that he could go through all this over again. Because he was polite, had no violent record, no felonies,a pregnant wife and two children. He was allowed to drive back home after paying the fines imposed. So we headed back home, the place I dreaded so much. We made it back safely to Virginia. I was in awe when some 10+ hours away it was warm and rainy, but back in Virginia it was actually freezing cold and snowing. We went straight to his grandmother's house. She allowed us to sleep on her floor. She made really thick palettes for us. We stayed there for about a couple of weeks until an apartment came through. As mentioned before, his grandmother was a devout Pentecostal. You know the type, believed in speaking in tongues, the Holy Ghost, communion, tarrying (tarrying is when a person says hallelujah so many times that they start speaking in tongues, as that's the only way to access the Holy Ghost). Women aren't allowed to wear makeup or pants. Must always wear prayer scarves. Refrain from consuming alcohol (except on communion, this particular church used

MD 20/20, which I found out later in life that it's the cheapest wine a.k.a. rot gut that is sold only in the ghetto) refrain from cursing, from divorce. You know the whole religious rap. But as holy as some profess to be, you must know them personally to know otherwise. Example, if she loaned my parents $100 cash, Greg or shall I say my mother would have to pay her back three times in food stamps. I.e. $100 cash equals 300 food stamps. So it would take my mom about 3 to 4 months to pay back $100 loan. It's sad to say but this woman became my new grandmother. I was uneasy around her, she had a way of throwing off on me,her own unique ways to slight me. Once she was praying for me and in the middle of the prayer she said "Oh Lord please bless this obese child" I thought to myself, I'm not a beast.I later asked my mom what did she mean by that. My mother told me that it meant I was overweight. I still didn't understand, I mean I was a little chubby but not severely afflicted by excessive weight. So I still didn't believe that this was applicable. There was another time when we were preparing to go to church and I was told by her that I was to take a wash up in the sink. I wasn't allowed to bathe in the tub or shower because that required too much water which caused her water bill to skyrocket. Needless to say I complied. This particular Sunday morning I guess I took a little longer to wash. So she rushed me, exclaiming in the hallway "Keifa, you gotta hur up or we gon be late fo church" (She spoke with a southern vernacular) "why you mov so slo"? So hearing this I hurried. I got out of the bathroom already dressed and ready to go. Well by this time her oldest daughter had arrived to drive us to church. So her daughter sent in her step granddaughter to retrieve us. This step granddaughter and I were the same age. So in front of her, she said "Kiefa now I no you didn't bathe gud cause you got out mutty quick,now gon back in dere and bathe gud" Even the name she called me was not proper. Clearly I told her my name as well as my nickname numerous times. The humiliation I felt, the humiliation of her rebuking me without cause and in front of my peer. The shame I felt within myself for not addressing her insensitive,inaccurate assumptions directly. I believe at this time in my life I was prime meat for manipulative people. I mean she was a church lady ,right? I did want to get caught up in the rapture, right? And if I chastised her for her misdeeds, God would surely see this and curse me I thought. She was a person who would cast God on you like a fishing rod. Let's say for example, her neighbor didn't speak to her one morning and two months later that same neighbor got sick or ran out of gas or what have you. She would say that God was dealing with them because they shunned her months ago.

Get what I'm saying, you didn't want to ever cross her, even when she was wrong. Because in her beliefs God would get you! And who wants that? She routinely spoke about the antichrist and the end of the world. She often told me that if I wasn't saved, I would be left on earth when the rapture came. To face the antichrist and die in the name of Jesus by beheading. So of course I wanted to be saved,I don't know about you but I really want to keep my head. But to be saved I had to be baptized in Jesus name and speak in tongues before the age of 13. Because once I was 13 every sin I commit God would hold me accountable. And this would greaten my chances of being sent to the lake of fire. So the first chance I got I was baptized at her church. One day, I started thinking about how much I love God and how much I wanted to be caught up in the rapture. The year 2000 was fastly approaching so I didn't have much time. And of course the preacher screaming into the microphone from the pulpit (pull pit) wasn't helping. I made a split second decision to be baptized that day, no exceptions! My mom wasn't present and I didn't ask her first because the Holy Spirit waits for no one. My soul needed to be saved pronto. In the prayer line, I let the preacher know that I wanted to be baptized in Jesus name. He blessed me, asked my name and who I came with. I thanked him, told him my name and let him know that I was mother so-and-so's granddaughter. So a short time later he made the announcement that I was going to be baptized in Jesus name, gave the congregation my name and told them that I was mother so and so's granddaughter. I went back to my seat to wait for an usher to take me to the baptismal pool and help me get prepared. Well wouldn't you know that my so-called grandmother went to the preacher and whispered something into his ear. I would say in about a minute or two the preacher made another announcement. He apologized to the church and made a correction. "Miss Robinson is getting baptized today and she is not mother so and so's granddaughter but her grandson's girlfriend daughter. Mother so-and-so is just watching her over the weekend" And the cobra strikes again! She practically begged me to call her grandma. She said that I was her granddaughter. According to her it didn't matter whether it was biological or not. It didn't matter who "put da bun in da oven, all dat matters is who's tendin to da bun"so she said. When I heard the preachers' correction, I immediately became flushed with embarrassment. In front of the whole congregation ,really? Nonetheless I still got baptized that day.

Another peculiar thing is that periodically she would cook food for my siblings and I. Like any child my age I loved sweets. She had this really and I mean really sweet apricot preserves that she made especially for us children. One day we, meaning myself and my two baby brothers ate some of her specially reserved apricot preserves. Not long after we left her house my brothers and I developed flu like symptoms. Headache, joint pain, eye pain, fever, vomiting, diarrhea and chills. I mean we were out of it! My mom viscerally took my brothers to the ER as they were younger than me and obviously in more danger. I toughed it out. My mom's boyfriend thought that it was just a 24-hour virus and I agreed. So anyways my brothers got IVs and medication, but the ER doctors were baffled because they couldn't figure out exactly what was causing the illness, even after standard blood test. So they gave scripts to ease the symptoms and told my mom to keep them well hydrated and bring them back immediately if the symptoms worsened. I myself was actually cold in the middle of July, in the South! It must have been at least 95° out but in the midst of this I was craving for the sun to shine on me to warm me up. That was the first time I had ever been this sick in my life! Come to find out some years later that my pseudo-grandmother had a life insurance policy on me and my brothers valued at $10,000 each! And to add insult to injury on this policy guess what my relationship was to her? Her granddaughter!

Really? I'm was her granddaughter when she hoped to profit from my death. But in church I was her sons friends, neighbors, stepsister's, cousin's, stranger child. A bit of an exaggeration but you get my point. And many years later I couldn't help but wonder was I poisoned? I've watched so many crime shows on discovery ID since to know that we had the classic symptoms of arsenic poisoning. According to toxicologist ,arsenic wouldn't show on standard blood tests. I've also watched enough of those shows to know that we shouldn't be so quick to trust any old lady claiming the glory of God! What a hard lesson for me to learn but I learned!

I've always wondered why I was spared? What was my Deen or purpose in life? Even in my preteen years I continued to feel like an outsider looking in. Even at school amongst my peers I found no relief. I recall my classmates particularly the black girls taunting me often. "You shop at Kmart, what kind of shoes are those?, you need a perm, you a nerd" So I had my mother at home calling me "fatty, fatty 2 x 4", her boyfriend calling me "pig nose" and my classmates verbally abusing me, oh my God why? I remember once when I was in the lunch line at school.Now if you ever saw school children in line waiting for lunch, you would know that it ain't pretty. Pushing, yelling etc. Anyways I was in line and someone pushed me, accidentally or intentionally I'm not sure. The force of that push caused me to bump into someone else. That person then pushes me back into someone else, that someone else pushes me into another person.And the next thing I know a group of children have encircled me pushing me from one person to the next.

Meanwhile the teachers and lunch ladies noticed nothing.Tired of being their human piñata, I scream "Leave me the fuck alone" whilst throwing blows. They dispersed afterwards to get their lunch and acted as if nothing happened. I got my lunch,sat down at a table to myself and didn't eat.After a few minutes I got up and walked fastly to the bathroom where I cried. There was another time when all the girls in my class teamed up against me. There was this one girl in my class, I'll call her LC. She thought she was all that and then some, the cats meow some would say. She was short, with the light complexion, very short hair that was always curled just right, new sneakers that were never dirty, the newest clothes. Whatever the fad was she wore it. She went for bad, ghetto to the max! She was the ringleader of her little clique. A bunch of girls that followed her around and acted as if she was their God. It seemed that they would die for her if she asked them to. They followed her blindly. There was another girl in my class who was equally as poor as us all but she showed her poverty just as I did, I'll call her CS. CS and I became friends. Anyway on days I came to school we got along well, like sisters. On days I didn't come to school she would talk about me with the other girls. So because of this we were friends and then not friends you may know the cycle- on-again off-again. This one day all of us girls had a bathroom break. Well LC got into the bathroom and started verbally degrading me. Saying things like I can't dress, I got nappy hair, I look like a monkey. I retaliated by calling her a geek. I know, I know, calling her a geek was weak. But I wasn't in a rush to fight and I knew that she didn't know what a geek was. So I called myself playing it safe while still saving face. She became irate and asked "What's a geek"? And then said "You a geek"!

Hearing the commotion, her posse came to her aid. Seeing them she mustered the courage to push me and I pushed her back. Her and I got into a shoving match. I heard her clique in the background saying "Un uh don't nobody fuck wit Shawnda". By this time our pushes became hits and I had trapped her in a stall, where I was getting the best of her. So each of the girls from my class ran up and hit me in my back while I was busy fighting LC. The bell rung and each girl ran out of the bathroom so they wouldn't be late back to class. The last girl in line to punch me was my so-called very own friend CS. She giggled as she ran away and she had a very distinctive laugh. Did she think she would be "in" because of her betrayal towards me? Whatever the reason, I saw her as an complete rat every since that day. We ceased being frienemies.

Once LC's mom came to school to speak with the teacher. They were discussing LC's bad behavior and grades. Her mother was appalled that the teachers would address these problems. I, as well as the entire class could hear her replies. "My daughter dress good, I work two jobs so I can keep her looking good, I take care of my mine. She always wear new shoes and I keep her hair done"

Meanwhile Mr. Taylor (the teacher) is trying to explain to her that he's not trying to attack her motherhood, but that academically LC is performing very poorly. Hearing and seeing the mothers demeanor, her utmost ghetto-isms. I then clearly saw where LC got this ignorant and shallow outlook on life. Not to mention their lack of problem-solving and human relation skills. When I progressed to the next grade, I was elated. Now in the six grade I thought I wouldn't suffer with mistreatment by my peers any longer. The balance for me I guess was that my teachers loved me. They believed in me and didn't mind letting me know this. No matter what they seemed to view me as one of their brightest pupils. I myself knew that I could have mastered every subject in school. But there was an stronger, more evil force at work that wouldn't allow me to excel, my mom's boyfriend. My teachers of course didn't know this. So they were pretty baffled when I got C's or average grades. A lot of times I received D's and F's due to my poor attendance. In my middle school that was a large percentage of rich white kids. Children of doctors, lawyers, senators etc. Their homes cost no less than $200,000 which was considered pretty well-to-do in this city. I've always been a person who likes to observe. My environment, society, nature. A great deal of what I've learned in life comes from observation. I would see brand-new hundred thousand dollar plus imports pull up to the school. When these parents dropped off their children, I would see kids with plain blue jeans, T-shirt and old sneakers (I'm generalizing here). Point being, these wealthy kids or shall I say children of the wealthy, were not and I repeat were not label whores! They cared less about this designer or that designer and they could afford it. Meanwhile at this same school, a small number children from the notoriously dangerous and poverty-stricken Jackson Ward projects were bussed in. And some of these children were placed in my class. Oh no here we go again!

You can probably guess was started next. Yep they ripped on me because I didn't wear clothes they saw fit. The funny thing is that my clothes at that time were designer. My mom brought my wardrobe from the secondhand store. We lived in a somewhat Yuppie area. So all of the donated clothes were Bill Blass, Liz Claiborne, Eddie Bauer, Izod, Sasson, Ralph Lauren etc. But these children had only been exposed to clothes aimed towards the undereducated, underpaid and misguided demographic. There was this one big clothing brand sold only in the ghetto named Troop. Well they didn't know that Troop is what one would call a group of monkeys. Nonetheless I dealt with their periodic insults, they didn't compare to the trauma I was experiencing at home.

In my class, I gravitated to this one girl. Her nickname was Tae. She was a thin, frail girl with glasses. She always wore dresses, no makeup or chemical hair treatments. In getting to know her I asked "Why do you always wear dresses"?. She replied "I got to, my mom and dad are Pentecostal. So I can't wear pants, makeup or anything". I made her aware that I too was Pentecostal but my parents weren't that strict. I told her that her parents only did this because they loved her and were trying to raise her right. No matter how much I tried to change her feelings towards the strict religious discipline her parents were trying to instill in her, she didn't sway in her views. It's like she had started to despise her parents. Years later, when we were both in our late teens, I saw her strung out and tricking(prostituting). Her need to rebel, I believe is what ultimately lead to this. It's kind of funny because anyone who was an outcast, black sheep or what have you, seemed to be attracted to me. This one girl in my class who was the Satanists, tried to explain to me her views and why. I believe she thought she would amaze me somehow but I had at that age read books on many different religions. I was already aware of people who chose that path so I refrained from judging her beliefs.

So many characters who have come into my life. Some positive, some negative. I have always tried to learn something from each experience. I learned through attending this school that the poorer an individual is, the lower self-esteem they have. Which as a result caused them to want to wear the newest clothes, shoes and hairdo's. And I wouldn't consider this economically sound considering most of my black peers at that time lived in the projects. Here the rent was an average of $25 per month but it was crime-ridden, drug infested and just plain dire living conditions. But they didn't care as long as they looked good! How absurd!

There was this one boy, Tucci was his street name. I never knew his government. Every girl in the school had a crazy crush on him. Firstly, he was from New York, I think Brooklyn. And everyone knows that in the black community when you are from New York and move to the South you get major respect, just because. In the southern psyche there is something that allures us about the North. But most of us are afraid to actually move north. Secondly, he was light-skinned, had 2 gold teeth, dressed what we at that time called fly. He had designer clothes from New York that hadn't made it to Virginia by that time. He was cool as ice with this charisma that made you stop in your tracks to watch him walk by. Nice features, nice physique, a ghetto king he was at only 15 years old. Us girls didn't care about how academically adept he was or not. 15 years old in the seventh grade didn't matter to us.

So one day I came to school and the girls in my class that resided in the projects were sad and distraught. Finally I heard one of the girls say "I can't believe Tucci dead" What? No way, I thought to myself. How could he be dead? Not asking for further details from any of the girls, my friend and I chatted about it the rest of the school day. Not being able to get any more details because Tae and I were not a part of the "in" crowd. That afternoon at home I told my mother what happened to Tucci. At 6:00 PM she tuned into the news. There I found out the story behind what happened. Tucci was dating an much older woman in the projects where they lived. I believe she was in her early 20s, I forgot her exact age. This woman already had a boyfriend older than her, in his 30s. Long story short, the boyfriend came home to find Tucci having sex with his girlfriend. Tucci jumped out of the bedroom window. And the boyfriend chased Tucci out of the apartment with his gun and shot Tucci in the back. May Tucci rest in peace. In my humble opinion he didn't deserve to die, to be murdered like an worn racehorse. Though he may have been an misguided youth, let he or she without sin cast the first stone. Anyway the guy got time in jail, I don't recall how many years exactly. But I recall it wasn't that much time as the value of urban youth isn't considered that valuable.

I attended half of the sixth grade at this school. And then a great shift happened, we had to move yet again. Okay I was use to moving a lot by this time, but where were we moving to? My mom told me that we were moving to the east end, Churchill section of the city. Now I know you think what's so bad about an area called Churchill. I mean how crazy could it be with a name like Churchill. It got its name because it has the most churches compared to any other section of the city.Personally, I believe that we, the people, are the church, temple, mosque or synagogue. This area of the city was filled with devils. Demons ran that joint. Crazy thing is that some of those devils were themselves in the church. Anyhow I was petrified. Frankly speaking I didn't fit, I didn't belong. I contrasted with my fellow peers of the same or similar racial heritage. Amongst my fellow black folk I was an outcast.

Now what am I going to do? I must go to school but I don't like to fight. I had at that time decided that choosing the path of least resistance was the safest way. Walk away quietly and you can't get hurt, right? I've always been spiritual but now was my time to really talk to God. I couldn't change the path that was before me, I just had to walk it bravely. Simple and plain. What was I being prepared for next? A question I didn't have the wisdom to ask myself at that tender age. So one weekend we went to see the new house where we were going to be living. It was an quaint little pink house on 25th St. It was reportedly built by hand by ex-slaves in the late 19th century. When I walked in, I had this heavy feeling. I didn't know why but it was heavy. I'll get deeper into that later.

I attended Mosby middle school for the remainder of the six grade. My teachers were fine and I liked them. They liked me in return. Mrs. Whitlock, my social studies teacher and Mr. Hicks, my math teacher were my favorites.

These two would always drop jewels or shall I say give wisdom to us underprivileged children. My classmates didn't seem to hear them or care but I did. When they said that we could be anything we wanted to be, I believed them. Going to this school I first had to lose fear of fighting. Secondly I had to act cool and not worried about shit. Basically I had to become an actress! Thirdly I had to get use to ghetto nicknames and I mean ghetto. Bread, cheeseburger,coo chie,rip,boom,bam bam,zo. These are actual names of people I knew. I couldn't tell you their government names to save my life.

Truly when teachers did roll call,I didn't know who those people were. Johnny Evermost, Shante Treebranch,who is this? Who is that? I would ask myself. After some time I got my own name. I was called cool wave! I was called this because I always had my hair brush to the back like the singer Sade. Whom I thought was one of the classiest most beautiful singers of that time. What was wrong with that? What was wrong with natural hair?

My female peers had their hair fixed to the hilt. Finger waves, perms, stacks, hair shaved off on one side, weaves you name it, they had it all at 11, 12 years old. The boys and girls would take turns insulting me. My shoes,my nails,my clothes and my hair were all up for discussion. My clothes were secondhand, my nails were natural, not airbrushed artificial tips, my shoes $12 soda pops that my mom brought from the local drugstore/clothing store. I recall once when my teacher, Mr. Hicks had to leave the class room for a moment. The majority of the class took their turn bussing (joking) on me.

I didn't know what to do but ignore them. I was more fearful of these children than the previous bullies at my old school. These bullies were quite a bit more dangerous. So I just stared blankly at the floor. This one boy, Alfonzo was his name, said loudly "Look y'all she praying". And indeed I was, how did he know? Did he feel my energy? I prayed with a heavy might that they shut up and leave me alone. Not a few seconds later Mr. Hicks walked in. Thank you God, thank you! Surprisingly the bullying at this school was pretty light.

I didn't get into fights every day, week or month for that matter. As I thought I would be before attending this school.

Though there was this one girl who wanted to fight me. Shawna was her name. I'll never understand why. I never associated with her or even spoke to her. I recall one day when her and her crony followed me home threatening to beat me up. In a poor neighborhood in the South you can always bet that you'll find empty 40 bottles somewhere near. So being the actress I was, I picked up one of those bottles by the neck and tapped the bottom of the bottle on the curb.Causing it to break at the bottom leaving sharp jagged glass exposed. I threatened to fuck her up if she came near me. She and her crony, who was quiet, continued to follow me but kept their distance. So when I got home I told my mother what happened and she urged me to tell my teachers at school. I heard that one before.That was as deep as it went with my mom. I later that day told my mom's boyfriend. He gave me pointers on how to fight, how to hit and where to hit. He informed me that street fighting wasn't pretty. He said that anything goes.Biting, kicking, scratching, gouging eyes, you name it.Thankfully though it didn't come to that.

Anyhow I managed to make some friends at the new school. The nerd crew, yep, I was part of that set. It was Tiffany,Shaquana and myself. Tiffany and Shaquana got good grades because they attended school every day. I on the other hand had potential to make good grades but didn't achieve it because of my poor attendance.

I've always believed in the power of prayer. I was honestly afraid of the girl who followed me home. She was quite taller than me and very rough appearing. One day she came to school with the cast on her leg and since that day she didn't bother me. Maybe she ran into her equal match.Or maybe she had issues at home.But whatever her dilemma was, I was happy when she eventually moved before the end of the school year. Thank you Creator once again.

Funny thing about my life is that I always seemed to live a double life. At school the children thought I was this nerdy square who had a plush life.With a decent mom and dad (they thought Greg was my biological father) little house in the ghetto, nice car. But they didn't know the horrors I was experiencing at home. Being raped, sodomized, seeing my mother be beaten up and tortured, not always having food. There were times when my parents sent me to the store to boost so that we could have dinner. Imagine a young child stealing to feed her family. There were times when our electric got shut off. I often found myself doing homework by candlelight. And I hated when our water got turned off. For me taking a bath was my sanctuary, the only place where I could have some peace away from everyone. I did most of the diaper changing,washing clothes and chasing behind my siblings,etc. But times when we got our water turned off for nonpayment, I had to walk to the local gas station or the side of someone's house to fill up no less than four empty gallon jugs with water. By this time I was use to being their workhorse. Use to doing arduous task while they comfortably sat at home. Once in a while I questioned their concern. Why can't they help me? Why can't Greg do this? But mostly I chalked it up telling myself that this was only making me stronger. One day some good will come from all this pain I thought, for the Bible told me so! There were times when I carried guns for Greg. He didn't always keep a car, so when he didn't and he decided that he wanted to walk to the corner store to buy beer. He would use me to carry his gun. So if the police ever stopped us, he wouldn't get a concealed weapon charge. Which is a felony in Virginia. Me, believing in fairytales thought no problem I'll carry his gun so that he won't go to jail, he's a prophet. How could I not assist a man of God?

I grew up battling my own perceptions, my own emotions, my own intellect, my own realities. How could I think he was a man of God, when I knew the evil works he casts? Then I thought of Job, King David and so many others in the bible who were imperfect.Yeah crazy I know,but that made sense at the time. Anyhow he taught me how to shoot guns. I've shot 25, 380, 40 and 9 mm calibers. He had also owned pump shotguns as well as tech nine's but I have never shot those. We lived in a bad neighborhood and I was convinced that we needed weaponry. Plus according to him, we had to protect ourselves from evils of the end times. He gave me examples of how in the past believers were persecuted and beheaded. This is the twisted climate I grew up in, interpersonal espionage, paranoia and manipulation. Yes he was bad but the world was worse I thought. In a strange way I saw my own abusers as the only friends I had.

When returning home from school each day, I had about 20 minutes to get home. One or two minutes late and I would have some explaining to do. Five minutes or so and I got a beating. They convinced me that this was normal. They only wanted to protect me, as I was often told. I envied other children who had normal appearing lives. Who could go outside and play, go to the movies or arcade, talk on the phone to friends etc. Keeping these horrible secrets I believed would earn me a special place in heaven someday.

It baffled me when I witnessed some of my male and female peers, bragging about how they sold drugs, beat people up or how much time they did in Juve. Was that anything to be proud of? Growing up poor, I myself was a part of the streets. And street life was nothing to embrace or boast of. No, I have never sold drugs. No, I have never sold my body. No, I have never used illicit drugs. But indeed I am aware and empathetic to the struggles of the ghetto. I've witnessed junkies smoking crack, heroin addicted pregnant prostitutes, dead bodies in cars, shot up over girls or drugs. There was this one girl in my neighborhood who was about one year younger than me. Whenever I ran errands I would see her. She always seemed to not like me and I wondered why. Why couldn't we be friends? Anyhow several months later she was found dead in a vacant building in my neighborhood. Only 12 years old if I remember correctly. It was soon discovered and released via the newspaper that she was addicted to and over dosed on heroin. She was also a prostitute. So tragic I thought. Maybe this is the reason why she wasn't friendly. And I am guilty of feeling sorry for myself!

At school not many boys paid me any attention. For the longest time I thought that I was ugly. My stepdad made sure to keep me aware of my Afrocentric features, as if it were a bad thing. My mother made me aware of my being chubby. I didn't entertain the idea of being attractive until some years later. When I was 19, I was leaving out of a store and a tall, beautiful drag queen looked at me and said "Ooh girl you're so cute" I couldn't believe that he was talking to me. But I then accepted his compliment to be genuine because he had no sexual interest in me.

However I did have secret crushes. There was this one boy named Charles, I really liked him because he had braces. How nerdy of me right? He didn't even notice me. I knew that I could never have a boyfriend. There was another boy who I thought was cute. I don't even remember his name as he was barely at school. He smiled at me and I would smile back. So one day I was walking home from school and he happened to be walking the same route with his girl cousin. He saw me and walked towards me. I thought nothing of it as he walked beside me conversing. He asked my name, where I lived, how old I was etc. General questions to know me better. So in the midst of this question session, he grabbed a hold of my hand. I immediately pulled my hand back and ran away from him shouting "Don't touch me" with tears in my eyes. He must have thought I was crazy. But he didn't understand what it was like to be me. The slightest touch from a man or boy and I thought the worst.

I could like a boy from afar but intimacy was my biggest fear. At one point in my youth I questioned my sexuality. Am I suppose to feel this way around the opposite sex? If I like a guy is it normal not to want to have sex with him? My girl peers didn't seem to have that dilemma. Am I gay? Am I straight? Am I asexual? After that day I stayed away from him. No more smiling, speaking or flirting. I didn't want him to misconstrue my childish flirtation for anything sexual. It wasn't really anything to worry about because from that day forward when he saw me in the hallways of school ,he gave me the most peculiar look.

When I was a child for several years I slept walk. I didn't know and am still not sure what it means but it didn't become a big issue. It was never a danger to my safety. When we first moved into that neighborhood and into that house.,I vividly recall praying to God that my family and I were protected. And if by chance danger was lurking that I would be made aware of it through vision. Being southern and Pentecostal, I believed strongly in visions. Some people say psychic but whatever it's called I'm convinced that some have this ability. There is a reference to it in the movie "Eve's Bayou". I suggest watching it one day if you haven't already. One night I had the oddest dream. I dreamt that someone broke into our house and stole our valuables. I couldn't shake this dream, so I told my parents. I didn't think much of it until two days later. We were coming back from the movies on a weekend night. We pulled up on the side of the house and Greg noticed that our back door had been kicked in. He drove to the nearest payphone and my mom called 911. We waited outside for the police. When they arrived, they went inside and did a sweep of the house. They came back outside and let us know that no one was inside. The police informed us that we were smart not to go into the house without their assistance. Our back door was off the hinges. Our TV, VCR, VHS tapes, moped and coats all were gone. You're not going to believe this but they also took our food from the freezer and fridge. The only thing that was left in the fridge was some uncooked fresh collard greens and a half gallon of milk. How much of a savage can one be? The police informed us that they would make a report and then we had to call the landlord to fix the door. They also gave us the contact number to the Red Cross to see if they could assist us in any way. My mother contacted them and they said generally they didn't help but because we were homeless and my mom had young children they would sponsor us in a hotel for a few days until our door was fixed. That was the good old days, now I don't think we would get any assistance. After Katrina, September 11, etc. It would take something much more drastic to get any help. They'd probably would laugh at us nowadays. As you may have already figured they never caught who broke in.

You know the street code,no snitchin. But rumor has it that my mom's nephew and his best friend were the ones who broke in!

When we settled in the hotel room, my mom brought to my attention that I had that dream a couple of days before. It had slipped my mind by then. My mom's boyfriend went directly to the payphone at the nearest convenience store and called his grandmother. He could have just used the payphone in the lobby or better yet the phone in the room. But he was always paranoid that someone was tapping the phone. So he switched payphones regularly. What was he so paranoid of? Only he knows the true answer to that question.But I have my theories. He greeted his grandmother and told her how someone broke into our house and that I had dreamt of it days before. At that moment I honestly felt that I had some value.

Living in that house wasn't the easiest task. Now only because of the obvious reasons, but because there was something dark in that house. Some people say haunted or para-normal activity. I say dark and mischievous energies or entities. When random objects would start falling off of the mantle I thought nothing of it. It happened once and I thought okay it's just vibration from somewhere that's causing this. I would go to the foyer and place the object back. Several minutes later it would fall again. So I moved the figurines from the mantle to the China press. From that location this still would happen. Having never experienced this phenomena before I still thought nothing of it.

In school one day casually conversing with my friends. One asked me "What house do you live in again"?"The pink house" I replied."The pink house, girl yo house haunted". She went on to say how it was vacant for a long time and that her, another friend and their boyfriends broke into the house one day to drink and smoke weed. She said that while in there strange stuff happened. They heard strange noises and sounds but they didn't think much of it until a voice whispered one of their names, while they were quiet. They quickly left out and came to the consensus that the house was haunted. Now being that she openly stated that they drank alcohol and smoked weed, normally I would have attributed this to a drug crazed hallucination. But being that I however wasn't under the influence of drugs or alcohol. And I was having similar experiences I quickly registered that this was the answer to the lingering question, of why these objects continued to fall without cause.

I remember this one time on Christmas night my mom, her boyfriend and my siblings were out visiting his relatives. I was left to stay at home by myself because I was pregnant. After a short time I heard keys as if someone were opening the deadbolt lock on the front door. I heard my mom's voice call my name. I quickly ran to the front door to greet her, as I was very fearful of being home by myself in a haunted house. I got there in a matter of seconds and lo and behold,there was no one there! Know was this incident an actual haunting or my mind playing tricks on me? You be the judge, I have my beliefs. And one thing is for certain, the objects falling was not a figment of my imagination.

Growing up in the environment I lived in, as you could have guessed. I was constantly depressed. I first thought about taking my own life at about 12 years old. The event that first made me actually try was when one night I finished all my chores, I mean everything.I scrubbed the floors, cleaned the kitchen, the bathroom, their bedroom, dumped the trash.I pretty much cleaned the entire apartment. I was a big lover of biblical movies. Jesus of Nazareth was on television. My stepdad was sitting down watching it. So I sat down to watch the movie as well. Shortly after, my mom came over to me saying "Bitch you better get yo ass up and do something". I informed her that I had finished all of my task and that I really wanted to watch the movie. She came over to me, got on top of me and pinned me to the floor by holding her thumbs against my throat. Saying in a malicious tone "You better get from beside my man" Meanwhile I was gasping for air and "her man" was just sitting there watching the whole situation. After I kicked for a while, maybe a minute, give or take a second, but it felt like forever and a day. She let go of me and I got up trying to catch my breath. I ran out the back door and contemplated the next move to make.My first thought was, I'm going to call the police and tell everything that they've done to me. And then I thought to myself, my mom tried to kill me, my stepdad rapes me but if I call the police they're going to jail and then my siblings and I are going to be stuck in foster care. In foster care I was told, by them of course, that things would be worse than I could ever imagine. I was told that I couldn't go to any authority because "The system is not going to turn on its self" The only option I thought plausible was for me to take my own life and be done with all the physical and emotional torture.

My mother came to the back door and beckoned me to get back into the house. I was just standing on the back patio crying. When she called me I said to her sobbing "I didn't do anything". As if I had did something wrong that would have been an acceptable punishment. Anyhow I went back in but I had my mind made up,I was going to kill myself. So I calmly walked in and apologized to my mom. I knew I did nothing wrong but I guess that was my way of making peace. I went into the bathroom and got all the pills in the medicine cabinet. Ironically the only things available were vivarin and regular strength Tylenol. Vivarin was an caffeine tablet on the market that was formulated to keep a person awake. I was young, silly and depressed. I believed that if I took more than recommended of anything,I would surely die. I don't recall exactly how many Tylenol and vivarin I took but I remember it was all that was in the bottles. I went to bed expecting to be dead at any moment. After about 45 minutes I started to feel sick. Severely nauseated, drowsy with blurry vision and a somewhat detached feeling. I felt like I was in a dream state. Yes, I'll be dead at any moment now I thought. Seconds turned to minutes, minutes turn into hours and the next thing I know it was light outside. What? How could this happen? I certainly felt sick enough like I was going to die but strangely I couldn't fall asleep. That was the most miserable feeling. That morning my mom noticed that I was lethargic. So she asked me what was wrong. I told her that I took some pills and I wanted to die.

So she went and informed her boyfriend of what I did. He was in the midst of getting ready to visit his grandmother. In a flippant manner he said "I don't care, she gonna do dumb shit let her then." Looking back I realize that it would have benefited him had I died. I was walking evidence. Meanwhile my mom was fussing at me. Calling me stupid saying that I really didn't want to die and asked me how many pills I took. After some time they both were ready to leave. They told me that I couldn't go because of my appearance from the pills I took. I vividly remember me standing in the threshold of the back door watching them get into the car. As Greg was getting into the driver seat he looked at me. We made eye contact and he coldly rolled his eyes at me as he got into the car. He then drove off. I had another failed attempt when I was about 13. Greg was one of the coldest, hostile and violent people I have ever personally known and hopefully will ever meet. His evilness is enough for anyone to come into contact with for a lifetime. He had a way of making someone scared to cross him. And crossing him meant standing up for yourself, seeking justice, being honest and forthcoming about all his misdeeds. He had the ability to bring fear without even speaking words.

He had this very small scar/keloid on his forehead from a fight that he got into in jail. He was always stressing about this miniscule scar. My mom has permanently deformed ears because of him, but he, a so-called man, was spazzing about a barely noticeable scar. What a cookie-cutter narcissists.

So one day out of frustration he went to the liquor store and brought whiskey and beer. He then went to the pharmacy and brought Tylenol, sewing needles, a razor and black thread. When he got back home he went directly into the bathroom, leaving the door open. He called me and told me to sterilize the sewing needle by inserting the tip of the needle into the fire from the kitchen stove. Once sterilized I took it back to him, he then asked me to thread it for him. And I did so. Out of pure curiosity, I asked what was he going to do. His answer shocked me. He was going to cut out the scar. Right in front of my eyes he took the blade from the pack. By this time half of the liquor was gone. He began cutting through his very own flesh. He told me to leave. But a short time later he called me back to bring him a beer. By this time he was sewing the incision up.

When you see a person standing in front of you sewing their own self-inflicted wound without flinching, it is downright horrifying. For some reason it made me think about the early Terminator movies with Arnold Schwarzenegger. If Greg could be this emotionless, detached android type being. Then imagine what more brutal damage he could inflict on me without even blinking. The image of what I witnessed that day is forever etched in my mind.

As I got older the rapes got more frequent. I actually got numb to being raped. My mind was in another place while these attacks took place. I felt trapped, powerless, unloved and hopeless. The difference in the rapes is that it shifted from being anal to vaginal. This started when I was about 12. There is so much that I have intentionally blocked from my mind. Just by me writing down what happened to me makes me want to cry. Some days I feel that I can't go through with this. At times I just want to forget everything and everyone that caused me this tremendous pain. But I know I cannot. I must push through this agony, I must endure. If my candor about my abusive child and early adulthood can help me to heal, so be it. Even more important, if sharing my life story can help other girls and women heal then this is worth it. I would have found my purpose. I can't tell you the exact day or time when the rapes became vaginal. Honestly in my opinion it is irrelevant. All I know is that it was displeasing, painful and disgusting either way. Sometimes he used condoms, sometimes he didn't. But times when he didn't, after he was through raping me, he would make me wash as he watched . He didn't want to take a chance of leaving any DNA. Dena is what he called it. He learned that phraseology from being incarcerated. I recall once when he got out of jail, he came home and told my mother and I about some white guy who was locked up for raping his three-year-old niece. What got me upset is that he seemed to think that he was better somehow. Yeah okay raping a nine-year-old has honor, but a three-year old, oh my God what a monster! In his dreams and our nightmares!

As one might imagine, having sexual contact regardless of age or non-consent inevitably lead to pregnancy. At the age of 13, my period stopped. Completely aloof, I had no idea what was going on. One month went by and then two,three, four. I believed that it was just some sort of female problem. So I really didn't pay it any attention. Finally one night as I'm lying in bed on my back, I felt an flutter & then another flutter. Oh my God I thought, something is moving around in my belly. I thought that this couldn't be happening to me. At that moment I had mixed emotions. A part of me was astonished to have a living being growing inside of me. Another part of me thought what am I going to do? I'm so young. How will I support a baby? How will I explain this to my schoolmates? The following day I finally told my mom that I had missed several periods. She took me to the ER later that night. There the doctors asked their usual questions. They took blood and urine samples. The doctors came back a short time later and confirmed to my mother that I was pregnant. Something I had already speculated. After leaving the hospital my mother started her round of questioning. It baffles me how my mom loved to play psychological games with me. "What did you do"? "Who is the father"? "How long have you been sexually active"? "What are you going to do with the baby"? She put on the most straight laced and sincere face might I add. Like she really didn't know. All in the name of toying with my mind. How could she question me this way?

Going to school and not every day, was as social as I was allowed to be. I was timed from school to home. I was timed when I ran errands. Most relevant and shameful on her part, is that I told her what he was doing to me years earlier. If my mother was hurt to know that her boyfriend impregnated me, I really didn't care. I guess subconsciously I believed that she deserved any negative or hurtful emotions that came with my pregnancy. She had let me down as a mother in the worst way. And honestly I had an underlying hate towards her for that. But nonetheless out of fear and retribution from Greg, I played the game along with her. "Oh mom, just some boy from the neighborhood" "It only happened once and I want to keep the baby" I replied. Any pacification to shut her up. Meanwhile I'm was filled with anxiety. Wondering what is he going to do, what is he going to say, how is he going to react? When we got back home my mom told him the news. And bizarre as it may sound he asked me the same questions. Crazy right! He knew very well that he was the culprit. So I responded with the same answers as I did with my mom.

Later that night he cornered me and asked me how long had it been since I missed my period. I informed him that it had been about four months. He then asked me why I didn't tell him sooner. I let him know that I thought nothing of it. (A testament to my innocence and gullibility). He then told me that I had to have an abortion. I pleaded with him not to kill my baby. He still insisted that I have an abortion. I told him that I didn't think that God would ever forgive me if I murdered my baby. He then told me that he couldn't take the chance of people talking and asking too many questions. For that moment I gave up my argument. In my heart believing that somehow, someway I wouldn't have to have an abortion.

So the following business day my mother started making calls to local women's clinics. She wanted to gather details and pricing information for abortions. By then I believe I was about 4 1/2 months into gestation. Which means legally the baby was considered an fetus or human.

I still could have an abortion but the price increased a great deal because of this. I don't recall the price exactly. But I recall my mom telling him that it was in the neighborhood of $400 or $500. An considerable amount of money then and even now. Mind you, at that time, my mom was on welfare. With an monthly income of around $350 a month. He wasn't working as you could've guessed. So in a twisted way being impoverished actually worked to my advantage.Greg vowed to hustle up the money for the abortion.

Knowing that his primary concern was not to get caught for his crimes committed against me. I told him that I wouldn't tell anyone he was the father of my baby. And I begged that he at least let me carry the baby and then give it up for adoption. Surprisingly he agreed. Knowing that I had brought myself only a little time, I couldn't fully relish my small victory. My mother found me an Ob/gyn doctor very close by. As a matter of fact, he was just 1 block up the street from my house. Dr. Royal was his name. He and his wife (who was also a doctor), ran the practice. Dr. Royal was very strict with me. He explained to me that I was very high risk because of my very young age. He also informed me that not following the proper diet would exacerbate the risk. Which included but not limited to miscarriage, premature delivery, mental retardation, developmental problems, breathing problems etc. He only agreed to keep me as his patient if I vowed to cut out all junk food, not to be around secondhand smoke, reduce stress and stay away from other young people stuff that would jeopardize my baby's health. Which I did and stayed true to my vow. The sexual assaults became less frequent as I progressed in my pregnancy. Surprisingly he wasn't as mean to me either. My mother would come around when he wasn't around and say to me "You better hope you have a boy if you want to keep the baby, because he already told me that he wants another son" While pregnant I had this very lucid dream that I was raped by Satan. I guess that was a result of my deep, painful, traumatic experiences manifesting through my dream. My doctor calculated that my due date was July 4, 1992. Through ultrasound it was determined that I was having a girl. What am I going to do? I'm having a girl. There was no chance of me keeping my baby now I thought. Not long after I found this out, I had this very vivid nightmare. I dreamt that he molested my daughter. I woke up out of my sleep crying. My heart was beating fast. It took days for me to shake that nightmare. Never forgetting it, it was always in the back of my mind. Would he ever molest or rape his own biological daughter?

Greg would cook for me. He baked and broiled chicken, vegetables, rice. He actually made sure that I took my vitamins, drank milk, stayed calm, didn't do too many house chores. That was the most peace I ever had. His violence turned more towards my mother. She caught the wrath of his paranoia. So there were still stressing factors but I tried with all my might block them out.

The yelling, screams and cries of my mother. Even at the age of 13, I still lacked the heart to do something. I at that age blamed my mother for his violent outburst. Why does she not hold her head down in the presence of men? Why would she speak to a male coworker if she knows how much it upsets him? I didn't fully understand the significant horrors my mother suffered until I was older. When I myself suffered more from his torturous rage beyond the sexual.

My pregnancy wasn't really complicated. I followed the doctors' strict orders. I had the occasional morning sickness as my baby got bigger. No high blood pressure, gestational diabetes, swelling, preterm labor. I can say that I was truly blessed. As time drew closer to my due date, anticipation and anxiety weighed heavily on me. I really wanted to keep my baby. I wanted to keep the only person that would love me. Who didn't want to abuse or use me. Someone I could call my own.

He made me call adoption agencies. I intentionally foiled most calls. Hoping and praying that the agencies didn't answer their phone or something. This one agency I called, I don't recall the name.But the woman I spoke to was very pleasant. She had a soothing and caring phone demeanor. She asked my name and what I wanted to do. I told her my name, age, phone number etc. and that I wanted to give my baby up for adoption. She then asked my medical history, due date and what hospital I planned to have my baby at. She's then explained to me the whole process. I would call her when the baby was born then she would come to the hospital. Once there she would have me sign paperwork to waive custody of my baby. At that time she would take my baby to her potential adoptive family. She could not give me the name or address of the family but she did tell me that my daughter would be living in Fredericksburg, Virginia. I then would have 14 days to relinquish custody permanently or keep my child if by chance I changed my mind. As allowed by Virginia state law at the time. Afterwards there would be no other options unless my adult daughter would have decided to seek me out. As stated earlier this was not my desire, but I didn't have any other options.

My baby girl was born July 6, 1992. It's funny because I didn't know I was in labor. I believed I was just having some really big stomach pain that felt like menstrual cramps. I even took Tylenol, believing that Tylenol could take care of any pain. Silly me! As I lie in bed having extreme pain,Greg didn't know what to do. My mom rushed home from work.The next thing I realized, there was water gushing from my vagina and I started having these strange feelings there.I didn't know that I was dilating. I didn't realize what was happening until I got into the ambulance and one of the paramedics, (who was a guy) looked underneath my sheet. He made a face that showed utter disgust. He looked as if he was going to vomit in any minute. He then told the woman paramedic that I was crowning. The woman calmly and politely told me that she could see my baby's head. She also said that I needed to stop pushing until I got to the hospital. I tried very hard not to push but honestly that was the only thing that alleviated the excruciating pain. Once at the hospital it was straight to business for me. I automatically started pushing once I passed the hospital threshold. I was settled in the delivery room, which was set up like a bed room. My nurse told me not to push, that I had to wait for Dr. Royal to get there and that he was on his way. Well after such strong contractions, being fully dilated and pushing, my daughter was ready to come into the world and not wait another minute. So about 15 minutes after arriving and five minutes before my OB doctor walked in, my little girl was born.

She was so tiny and beautiful.Like an actual doll baby. A breathing, crying, eating one! When the nurse asked me if I wanted to see and hold my baby, I couldn't say yes quick enough. Mind you, I was at the hospital by myself. So that's how I was able to do so. I instantly fell in love with her. When the doctor arrived he informed me that I would need 2 to 3 stitches. Although small she was still too much for my underdeveloped body. She weighed a whopping 6 lbs. 5 oz. and 19 inches long. Later that night my mom, her boyfriend and my siblings made their way to visit me. At that time they didn't have a car. So they took public transportation. When they arrived they came bearing smiles, hugs, kisses and food. My mother went through great detail to let me know that it wasn't an easy task to reach me. She told me how they caught the bus halfway and had to take a taxi the other half. Then the taxi driver charged extra money because they stopped at Dairy Queen to buy me a burger and fries. Once at the Dairy Queen the prices of the food was more than they expected to pay.But they brought it anyway because there were no other stores open in that area. And they knew that I was hungry. After my mother finished telling me all this, I felt an overwhelming sense of guilt. Knowing how poor we were, how could I put them through even more financial hardship? Although happy to receive it, the food suddenly tasted like cardboard. My mom then let me know that she had called the adoption agency and that the following day they would be there to take my baby. I instantly got a lump in my throat so I just nodded my head in agreement. They then left, the total time for the visit was about 20 minutes. Being older and knowing a little how Greg thinks. I'm sure he coerced my mom to go through great lengths to make me aware of their inconvenience. And also most importantly make me believe that they cared for me deeply so I wouldn't tell anyone that he (a man 15 years older,rapist and acting stepfather) was the father of my child.

He loved playing mind games like that ,and sad to say my mom was always by his side to lend a helping hand. The following day the nurses asked if I wanted to feed my baby, of course I agreed. The nurse brought in formula and asked if I decided to bottle feed or breast-feed. I let her know that I was giving the baby up. She asked once more if I still wanted to feed the baby. I let her know that I did. So she gave me a quick tutorial on how to hold, feed and burp her. These things I already knew from having younger siblings. But I didn't want to shut her down as I appreciated her concern and patience. She left the room and it was just me and my baby. I held,hugged, kissed and fed her. Looking into her little gray eyes. Praying to God with all my might that I would be able to keep her. I talked to her as if she understood every word I spoke.

Several hours later the woman that I was corresponding with entered my room. She was all smiles and very polite. I, on the other hand was all frowns, though I tried to muster a smile. She asked how I was, how was the baby and then she said that she was there to take the baby. But I would have to sign the paperwork first. I then asked where my baby would be taken to. She assured me that she would be in excellent hands with a family in northern Virginia who had a good education and income. I then asked her again the process. Once again she explained to me what I already knew but honestly I was trying to stall as long as I could. She then walked towards me, paperwork in hand. Smiling and eyeing my baby. Petrified to sign the paperwork and let her walk out with my baby. I told her calmly that I had to confer with my mom first. She then said that I had 14 days should change my mind. In my heart I knew that once the papers were signed, they (my mom and her boyfriend) could block me from getting her back. So I politely refused. She was very disappointed needless to say. Knowing myself, I would have regretted placing her up for adoption all my days. It would have eaten away at me day after day, week after week, month after month, year after year. She then said that she understood as she gave me her card and told me to call her when I was ready. She then informed me that she would drive to my location to pick the child up. When she left I recall crying and thinking to myself, What am I going to do?, How am I going to explain this? I love my child and I wanted the best for her but I couldn't stomach not having her in my life. Not knowing how she's doing, how she's being treated, her first words, her first teeth, her first steps. How would it affect her emotionally knowing that her birth mom gave her up? Would she forever hate me not knowing the intimate details?

The following day I was to be discharged from the hospital. By the grace of God I had a relatively smooth birth and my overall physical health was good. So the following afternoon my mom came to take me home. She asked did the people come to pick the baby up. I told her no and she asked why? I told her that I just couldn't do it. Once in the taxi she told me that Greg was going to be very mad at me. She said that I better apologize and beg him to forgive me. I asked my mother could I please keep the baby. She then said that it was up to him, what he says goes. My mother said that he might change his mind but I had to talk to him about it. When we got home I immediately went to him crying and pleading for him to forgive me because I couldn't sign the papers to give her up. I told him "I will take care of her, but please just let me keep her" He flatly and angrily said "Hell no, I told you what it was and now you wanna flip" I told him that the baby was still in hospital. He replied "I don't give a fuck but she ain't coming here" This dialogue went on over the course of about two days. At night I found myself praying to God very hard. Calling him by different names. Allah, Jah, Jehovah, Jesus, Yeshua. Whatever the proper name I didn't know and still don't know for that matter. But I just wanted my biggest prayer at that time to be answered. About one day later the hospital called my mother and informed her that she had to pick the baby up. Or they would notify the authorities and file abandonment charges against my mother, as I was a minor. It was on the weekend so the adoption agency was closed. Greg was livid, yelling at me saying that " You didn't win, the baby is still going to be put up for adoption. "So don't get too attached to her because she won't be here long" It's funny how faith works because not long before my oldest daughter's birth. Some church had given us garbage bags full of donated clothes. Inside the bags were some newborn baby clothes. Greg decided that he was going to take the clothes to the flea market and sell them. But before he did so, I took out two newborn sleepers, of course my parents were unaware of it. My mind set was just in case my little girl did come home she was going to need something to wear. He and my mom took a taxi to go and retrieve my baby. Before he left the house he said the usual. "I want this house cleaned from top to bottom" A small price to pay to be able to spend more time with my baby, even if it's just a day or so. When they brought her back home my mom was holding her. For the first time I might add. They had not previously saw or held her. My mother was actually dotting over her. Speaking of how beautiful she is.Greg however was just looking at her with a unreadable expression. But I'm almost sure he was thinking, she looks just like me. I asked could I hold her because I wanted to breast-feed her. My mother handed her to me and immediately I started feeding her. I've always believed breastmilk was best for a baby. My grandmother breast-fed all of her children. My mother breast-fed all of us, it may have been laced with liquor but nonetheless she did it. So I didn't want to break our maternal tradition. Suckling my first born was nothing short of a difficult task. I had no nursing pads, breast pumps or any other aides. Weeks passed and it seemed that he was growing attached to the baby. He would still occasionally throw in "I can make you give her up anytime I feel like it". I would humbly reply "I know".

To this day I'm still not sure exactly why he didn't force me to, but I would like to believe that it was my prayers and faith. Not long after, I had to give up breast-feeding. My breast became inflamed because of blocked milk ducts. So my doctor prescribed me some antibiotics and asked what my plans were for the future. I let him know that I intended on staying in school and going to college after high school. He then suggested some medication to dry up my breast milk. It would have been very difficult to breast-feed and concentrate on my studies. He let me know that I didn't have to breast-feed for the entire first year just as long as she got breast-fed for a minimum of six weeks. It would be equally as beneficial to her health. I felt comfortable with his suggestion and took the medication.

School started that September. Over the course of the summer break I had received my report card in the mail. It Indicated that I had failed the eighth grade. When I found this out I broke into tears. I didn't want to accept having to repeat the eighth grade. My mom and Greg saw my anguish and decided to file an appeal with the school board.

Honestly it was Greg's idea. After they filed the appeal a short time later the school board notified my mom that after careful consideration. As well as looking at my academic performance record when I was in school. And taking into account that I only stopped going to school because of my pregnancy. They decided to promote me to the ninth grade. They also stated that I only failed because of my attendance. My grades and disciplinary record were actually good. I was so happy and I thanked them both. Elated that I was on to bigger, better things or so I thought. Education had always meant a lot to me. And I intended on pursuing it to the highest level. I recall writing to various colleges inquiring about their various programs. I wrote to Rochester University in upstate New York, Virginia State University, Hollins University in Roanoke, Virginia. Rochester and Hollins actually replied inviting me to join them over summer break for two weeks to see if I liked their academic programs. I really wanted to attend Rochester because I wanted to get the hell away from my insane family atmosphere and Virginia. But also important, Rochester had archaeology programs, the best from what I've read. And I was big into being an archaeologist. Hollins was a great college as well. It was an all-girls college, which I thought increased my chances of being allowed to go. A slew of prestigious women attended and graduated from there. Women authors, Congresswoman, lawyers, doctors etc. As a Gemini girl I had many interests. I wanted to be a actress, rapper, archaeologists, astronaut, ballerina, nurse, poet or journalist. So I was for a short time indecisive. Through process of elimination I realized that I was way too shy to be an actress, rapper or ballerina. To fearful of heights and the unknown to be an astronaut. So after long consideration I decided that I wanted to be an archaeologist. It involved elements that appealed to me. Travel, discovery, culture, history, digging in dirt.I actually loved playing in dirt. Being an experimental gardener when I was younger. I once took a fresh green bean split it open and took out the seed. I planted the seed in a flower pot. I was amazed when new green beans sprouted. So when I started the ninth grade that September, I was very excited.I was one step closer to my peaceful escape. I was going to give it my all so that I would have the highest g.p.a., to solidify me being accepted into Rochester University. I would promptly get up each a.m. eager to get to school. As my electives I chose the JROTC program at Franklin military school which was annexed to my high school.I caught a lot of insults for "joining the beast".Greg called me every kind of sell out. I also took track and field. As Greg would have it, he found any and every way to throw blocks in my education.Yeah he helped me get to the next level and then pulled me down. I was due in school at around 7: 15 a.m. Monday through Friday. Well he decided that it was my obligation to take my baby brother to school each day. My little brother was due to school at 8:30 AM. So I had to wait until 8 AM to walk my brother school and that was about a 30 minute walk. He insisted that I walked back home first so now we're looking at 9:00 AM. Then I was allowed to walk to my school, which itself was a 20 minute walk. So each day I was getting to school between 9:30 AM- 9:45 AM. How could I make any progress? By the time I got to school I had missed about two periods. It was things like this that confused me a great deal. On one hand he helped me get to the ninth grade by telling my mom to appeal to the school board and on the other hand he blocked me from my high school education. Each day it was something different and each day I was allowed to leave home later and later. Until I eventually stopped going altogether. To cope with this great set back, I developed the mindset that I'll go back to school soon I'm only 14.

So the cycle continued. Arguments, fighting, screaming,rapes, verbal abuse. For me that was a normal way of life. When I was 15, I found that again I was pregnant. This time I went to a different doctor. I went to a clinic and the pregnancy was smooth. Strangely he mentioned nothing about abortion or adoption. When I found out that I was having a boy, he seemed pleased. I was determined not to give up my education so I asked my mother to enroll me in a city-funded public school especially for pregnant girls. It was located on the other side of town, the West end. Which meant that I was completely reliant on him taking me to school. The only other option was public transportation. Which required money that I didn't have. Being the power craved person he was, each day I had to beg him to take me to school and I did. When he picked me up in the afternoon he would drilled me. He asked "Who flirted with you. Who said something to you"?. At this school adults also attended who were seeking to obtain their GED's. So apparently he was fearful of someone, some adult getting close to me. I explained to him that the pregnant girls and adults were taught separately. So I had no real contact with adults outside of my teachers. Even with me explaining this in great detail numerous times. It made no difference and he stopped taking me altogether complaining about the gas he was using. I gave birth to my oldest son one month shy of my 16th birthday. At the time of my son's birth, my mother was incarcerated for shoplifting. I spoke to her over the phone while in labor at home. Greg wasn't home, he was doing some odd chores for his grandma. She paid him a few and I mean few dollars for this. That was about as deep as his providing went for most of the duration of my captivity. Anyhow when he returned home a short time later, I told him that I was in labor. He then rushed me to the ER. At the hospital I was left by myself. No grandmothers, no aunts, cousins, and of course no mother. No father or baby father for that matter. Once again I was feeling abandoned. Once my first son was born he brought me some comfort. But it only added to my despair when a girl from the school I attended for short time, was in the room next to mine having her baby. The difference, she had her mother, father of the child, family, flowers, balloons etc. I'll admit that I hid from her so she wouldn't see me. I did this by just staying in my room. Not walking the hallway or visiting the nursery. However my mom did call me a couple of times. Which surprised me as I didn't know you could make collect calls to a hospital. Now that I think about it, she must have linked the house phone account to the collect calls. Greg stayed far away from me when I was in the hospital giving birth to my first two children. He didn't want to be publicly seen with me if he could help it. Paranoid that someone would figure out that he is their father.

Having a son made me very proud.But all my pride could not compensate for the difficulty of having one daughter being potty trained and one newborn son. Not to mention I had dreams of returning to school to obtain my diploma. How could I manage all this? And in the midst of all this we were being evicted yet again. My mom was released from jail about two weeks after the birth of my first son. Shortly after we relocated to an area in the north side. It was a house that had been converted into two apartment units. By the time my son was three months old, I had landed a job at a local Burger King. I was elated to step into an adult role and provide for my children. I was so grateful that I was allowed to keep them. This job at Burger King I didn't keep very long. As a matter of fact it lasted only three days.It was very stressful. All the rules of how and how not to make whoppers, cheeseburgers etc. I can laugh about it now but back then I wanted to pull my hair out. I recall once when I was making a whopper in uniform fashion as I had been trained to do. But I made one blip, I mistakenly got carried away and put mustard on someone's whopper. I sent it out but got busted afterwards. Here came the manager, a tall, light-skinned black lady with a husky voice. "Shakira did you just put mustard on that whopper"? She then went into frantic mode attempting to catch the sandwich before it was given to the customer. But it was too late, the person got the sandwich and left. She went on to tell me how I must pay attention and I must never, ever, ever put mustard on a whopper unless a customer request it. She made me feel as if I was the cause of an apocalypse. I finished that day but I didn't return the next scheduled working day. I went to a local McDonald's up the street and placed an application. They called me back two days later. It was privately owned by a black Jamaican/Irish man. The wages were slightly higher than at Burger King. Which was a plus not to mention I could work more hours which I needed. I wasn't in school so my mom took care of my children while I worked. Granted when I got my pay all but $20 went to them. But it was a small price to pay to have my children. Worked and worked I did indeed, most weeks I worked 35+ hours which was a lot for a teenager. I had absolutely no social life, I wasn't allowed to. I was kept extremely sheltered. Whenever my employer needed someone to fill in they called me. Whenever someone needed a particular day off they called me. It didn't bother me, that was my only chance to be social. After all I was a cashier. A lot of college boys from the renowned Virginia Union, one of the first black colleges in America. Would come in the restaurant and flirt with me. Saying how fine they thought I was. That I looked like Gina (Tisha Campbell- Martin) and the singer Brandy. They would ask me if I had a boyfriend. Of course I lied and said yes, always. No matter how attractive, smart or polite the guy was. Taking someone's number would have been a death sentence. And believe it or not I also suffered from very low self esteem. I thought that I was the most unattractive girl. I didn't care how many guys paid me compliments, I didn't believe them. I always thought that they were after something and that there was no way they could have been sincere. This stemmed from years of my mother's boyfriend telling me how ugly I was.

Working was actually one of my escapes. A chance to feel normal. Except whenever he came inside the restaurant to check on me, it was very awkward. My coworkers all asked "Who is he"? I didn't know exactly how to respond. If I said he was my father they wouldn't believe me, he didn't look much like me. People always thought he was Puerto Rican, me black and Asian. Besides he was too young to be my father. So I told my coworkers that he was my brother and that we had different fathers. Some believed me but his over protectiveness caused some to look at him in a peculiar manner.

After working for a year I filed taxes. I claimed my two dependents and got a hefty refund. At least it was to me. I believe in the neighborhood of $1600. I recall shaking when actually received the check. Funny right? I thought that I could maybe escape politely with my dividends. He was on me like an hawk on his prey. No chance of escaping this time, but soon I thought, soon. So he had plans already for my refund. He was going to put down on a new car. Pre-owned but newer than the one he had. The total down payment was I believe $1300. With a monthly note of $300. Of course I was the person actually paying the note, as their monthly incomes combined equated to a little over that and they were responsible for paying rent.

To make matters worse, he rarely picked me up on time once he got the new car. Many nights I had to wait at the 24 hour gas station located across the parking lot, for a minimum of three hours. I recall one time I got off work at 11:00 PM and he didn't pick me up until 7:00 AM. A few times I walked home but it was quite a distance and through very dangerous territory. The heart of the north side ghetto, it wasn't delicate terrain to trek.Greg picking me up late became so much of a routine that one of my managers at McDonald's, Mike (a tall thin light-skinned Jamaican man) gave me a blank check to get a taxi home once. I guess he felt sorry for me, as I was one of the few dependable employees. I accepted the check only as a last resort. I've always been a prideful person and don't like handouts. I didn't use the check but I did show it to Greg when he finally arrived.

I went through verbatim of the dialogue exchanged between Mike and I. I was use to this, whenever anyone, particularly a guy said anything to me. I had to report the whole conversation. And I knew better than to not be completely honest. I saw what happened when he thought you betrayed him. So literally I was a good slave. Funny because I didn't see it that way then, I saw it as survival.

So many times I dreamt of a Prince charming. Someone I chose, someone I loved, someone who loved me, someone who could help me get out of my situation. But problem 1# A boy my age could be of no use to me as he himself was still dependent on his parents. Problem 2# How could I ever get to know anyone to the point of telling them my situation. Problem 3# A man who could help me would have been much older than me and I would have then become his slave.

So I figured that this master is truly evil but I didn't want to "jump into the fire from the frying pan". As my mother often said to me in reference to me leaving my hellacious environment. Hence he had invisible shackles on my mind and spirit.

While my mom was at home watching the children, I was working basically supporting the whole family. And Greg was out all day playing the field. I would find condoms in the car often. I didn't care as a matter of fact I hoped that he found someone. I wanted so badly for him to leave but that day never came. Him picking me up late went on for the whole duration of my employment at the restaurant. After about four months we had to move yet again. By this time his license had been suspended again. So he couldn't drive without the risk of being jailed. Which is something he absolutely hated. We moved into a pretty nice house in historic Jackson Ward. The problem was when I had to walk home around this time, I had to walk in the opposite direction. Which meant not only did I have to walk through rough territory but now I had to walk on the outskirts of the notorious Jackson Ward projects. The top most dangerous housing project complex in the city at that time. I recall reciting Psalms 23 every night I walked home. I worked night shifts and on weekends I wouldn't get off until 2:00 AM. Other days of the week I would get off at 11 o'clock or midnight. And trust me getting off a few hours earlier didn't make it any safer. I begged him to walk me home from the restaurant as I was petrified. He refused saying to me "Naw, you'll be okay those drug boys ain't gon fuck wit you, but if they see me they gon wanna start sum beef". He then offered me to carry his gun to and from work. I accepted but only carried it once. I just didn't feel comfortable having such a huge gun (a 357 with hollow point bullets) on my person. I knew how to shoot and where to shoot but the question was could I shoot someone? So that was the end of me taking his gun to my place of employment. Personally reflecting on these times, I think he was hoping that someone had kidnapped or killed me. He must have saw me as walking evidence. Someone who could cause him to lose his freedom at anytime.

As I got older, the attacks became more brutal. And the accusations more often. He would become so aggressive when he raped me that sometimes my vagina would remain swollen and sore for days. He would interrogate me for hours each night I got home from work. "Who said something to you, What did they say to you, How did they look, How old were they"? I recall once when he was going through his routine. We were in the kitchen and he picked up a steak knife and started thrusting it towards my chest. While questioning and accusing me this night he poked me with the knife right above my right breast. The wound started bleeding and he started crying. I also started crying touching the knife wound thinking I was going to die. He then ran out of the house saying that he was sorry. My mother came into the kitchen, looked at it and told me I was going to be okay. She then got some cotton balls, peroxide and Band-Aids to clean me up. A short time later he called my mom from his cellphone (yes, he had a brick cell phone I paid for) and asked my mom if I was going to be okay. She informed him that I was okay. He then asked my mom if I forgave him. My mom told him I did without question, without asking me. I still have a small keloid there to this day. It really baffles me how my mom always had his back no matter what ,even against her own children.

We were all (excluding my siblings who were in bed) sitting on the front room sofa one night watching television. And out of the clear blue he pushed and pinned me down. My mom then covered my mouth with her one hand and poured water out of a cup into my nose with the other. Needless to say I couldn't breathe. They seemed to think that my sheer terror was hilarious. Were they really trying to kill me? I don't think so but what they were trying to do was make me aware that they could, if they wanted to. I didn't find their stunt amusing at all. As a matter of fact, I wanted to kill them. After they let me up, I ran to my room crying. Lying in my bed I envisioned myself getting a hold of his gun while they were asleep. Shooting them both, running away afterwards and living on the streets. Please don't judge me. This memoir is about honesty and honestly that's what I felt at the time. But as I thought deeper, thankfully I thought myself out of that option. I decided that I couldn't throw my life away like that. I had already been to hell and back so heaven wasn't too far away! It turned out that I was several weeks pregnant with my second son when this transpired. Not long after that, I'm not able to recall the exact time but I'll give you an approximate of about two months. We were forced to move yet again. You must understand that he loathed paying bills of any kind. He would actually take rent,bill & utility money and buy himself jewelry. He was the most selfish person I pray that I ever encounter. He was selfish to the point of insanity.

So we moved into our new apartment and I was forced to quit my job. This apartment was located in the West end. His license was still suspended and I had no one who could take me to and from work. By this time my mother had gotten rehired at Hostess bakery. She brought home at least $500 per week. I was staying at home with my older children around this period and I was also responsible for my siblings. I did the usual washing clothes, helping with homework, walking them to and from school, cleaning the apartment, waiting on Gregs' every whim. I had at that point given up on attending high school. But I thought there's more than one way to skin a cat, figuratively speaking.I happen to like cats! So I mailed out a flyer that allowed the student to get their high school diploma at home. They sent me back a enrollment packet. Which required me to sign a financial contract and make a five dollar deposit. I did as they asked and received my school materials about two weeks later. My monthly payments were $25 a month. I thought surely he wouldn't mind paying such a little each month. The incentive was that he didn't have to worry about guys talking to me as he always thought and I would be getting my education right at home. Why would he mind that? Countless times he told me how I meant the world to him. How we were meant to be. How we knew each other in a past life. I could go on and on with all the lies that he told me. The usual bs you tell someone when you're trying to rock them to sleep. Sadly as a misguided, brainwashed youth, I believed his words instead of his actions. When one is caged and they think that they can't escape. It's human nature to trick oneself into believing that being caged isn't so bad. How could I make it on the outside anyway? Crazy thing is I recall him reading extensively, books on mind control and psychology. Silly me, never thought that he was applying some of these techniques on me. He was truly invisible. I spent so many formative years blindly walking in darkness. Letting his beliefs guide my soul into eternal emotional affliction.

For the first two courses I received A's. I was so excited, showing him and my mom my test results. Of course he wasn't amused. Soon my monthly installment was due. I told him as he made all of the financial decisions. My mom wasn't allowed to keep money either. "Okay" he replied. "I will get yo money order for you", "How much is it again"? Every day he left out I reminded him. Made note of it and gave it to him. I volunteered to walk to the nearest store and purchase it myself. All I needed was the money from him. I tried anything to solidify my bill being paid. His facade went on for a number of weeks. Meanwhile the school was sending notices that they wouldn't send any new courses until my past due bill was paid. So I gave up on that aspiration for then.

My third pregnancy was very stressful. I was 17 year old mother of 2 and pregnant with the third. Financially poor, abused, neglected and confused. I can't recall the countless times I ran out of the apartment with my mom calling me back to hell. She wanted me there but she did nothing to protect me.

Growing up music was essential for me. Essential for me to keep my sanity. I favored alternative rock, pop,rap,neo-soul, classical. Anyone who knows me, knows that I loved Prince's music. Most of his music resonated spirituality. I didn't find out until later, that he and I share the same birth date. I also felt some connection with Tupac, like millions of teens my age at the time. When most people analyzed Tupac ,they saw a gun toting, cursing, yelling thug. I didn't see that. I saw a misunderstood intelligent young man who had been pushed to the point of not caring because of all his past pains. I don't know how many times I felt like not caring. It seemed that by me caring, forgiving and loving my enemies (my so-called parents) was only causing me more physical and emotional pain. When Tupac died I actually cried real tears. I even contemplated naming my son after him. My second son was born a few months after Tupac passed.

A healthy baby boy weighing 8 lbs. 13 oz. I had him naturally. No pain medication or anything. I can't forget those contractions, even stronger than before. Once again I was by myself. No family, no extended family, no baby's father. When I first laid eyes on my son, I thought he was most beautiful baby. In my opinion, my son was so pretty that when they handed him to me, I double checked to make sure he was a boy.

The following day my mom and her boyfriend came around. To the hospital they were my parents, I, a teenage girl who got knocked up. I must have appeared to the staff as some kind of fast young girl who didn't have a clue who my sons' father was. Not the case at all. Strife continued, more drama ensued. Thankfully I was able to breast-feed my son with no complications. Having my children eased some pain but at the same time with each child, I felt that much more hopeless about my future. How can I move forward with my aspirations? How can I support them financially when I escape? How will my children feel not having their father around? How will I ever get married one day? What man wants a relationship with a single young mother? These are just some of the questions I had. So many I was afraid to answer. No matter what I tried to make myself believe. I was missing the key element, I didn't believe in myself. So having doubt, low self-esteem and fear caused me to stay in this very toxic environment. I had absolutely no support. My own mother had turned on me. I had told my mother how he was raping me years earlier. She only used this knowledge to blackmail him to stay with her. How could I have faith in any one? I guess you could say that I got use to being the sacrifice. My only concern was that he didn't abuse my babies and that they had an rapport with their father. No matter how he came to be their father, in my mind that was irrelevant. I just didn't want them to feel the same pain I felt not having my father in my life. I was so afraid that any other man who would be their stepfather in the future. Would only attempt to abuse, molest or rape my children,as what happened to me. I thought this guy is bad but he wouldn't hurt his own flesh and blood.

Several months after the birth of my third child, were yet again evicted. But this time we were forced to move into a hotel. They couldn't find an apartment prior to the eviction. My mom was forced to leave her well-paying job. He always feared that she was cheating on him. And this caused many arguments each night she came home from work. I recall once when he was torturing my mother and questioning her about cheating. He actually burned her with a clothes iron between her thighs. It looked to be second-degree from the way it blistered and oozed.

So we were all living in the one hotel room. It was me, my three children, three younger siblings, my mom and her boyfriend. It was quite expensive. We paid $275 a week. Now when I say we, I'm speaking of my mother and I. By this time she and I were working together. We actually had two jobs each. One at Bob Evans. My mom was a cook and I a prep chef.Our other job was at Bojangles fried chicken. He made us work together so I could watch my mother and report to him if she flirted with any guys. He was responsible for taking care of the children. By this time our money was used to purchase him a Lincoln Continental town car. It was valued at $35,000 at the time. I say purchased him the car because my mother wasn't allowed to drive. She knew how but her license was suspended because of him. He would drive on suspension and then whenever he was stopped, he would tell my mom to switch seats with him before the police got to the car. In return this caused my mom to be ticketed with every driving offense he committed. These tickets over time accumulated and forced DMV to revoke her license until all fines were paid. He vowed to pay them off for her as he was the true culprit but he never did. And I didn't know how to drive. He had promised me since around the age of 13 to teach me how to drive which he didn't. So my mother and I were working two jobs each while he was out roaming the streets. We paid for everything. The rent, food, gas, car note, and any other necessities. He would pick us up from work hours late. Sometimes me and my mom would walk home. We fussed about his wrongdoing the whole way home. Sometimes when we got back home, he still wouldn't be there. I would ask my little brother if they were okay and he said that they were fine. I then asked how long had his dad been gone. He informed me that he hadn't been back since he had taken us to work. My mom always made sure she brought home extra food each night. At the end of the night, food that didn't sell would just be thrown away. My mom had no qualms about asking the manager if she could take it home. My mom was always a hard worker so management didn't mind. Me, I couldn't begin to ask. I had so much pride. When he got back later that night my mom asked where he had been. He told her that he ran out of gas and got stranded. He got angry at her and said "Damn you act like I ran out of gas on purpose, you don't even care about what I've been through". I believe he got to my brother for telling us that he hadn't been home. As every day after that whenever I asked my brother he always said yes. I didn't find out the ugly truth until a while later. And boy was it a hard pill to swallow. One bright sunny afternoon, he had picked us up from job number one, which was just five minutes away from the hotel we were staying in. Usually he would bring the youngest children with him to take us to work but this day for some reason he didn't want to.

Anyway when we pulled up back from work, we got out of the car and some lady with a clipboard came walking up to us. She said she needed to ask us some questions. She identified herself by name and title. She was a social worker from C.P.S. My first thoughts were okay, we'll talk to her, let her speak to the children. She'll see that they're not abused in any way. She'll see that they're intelligent, well fed, joyous children and be on her way. If you don't know by now, Greg was a complete hotheaded. He said things to her that were hurtful and unwarranted. He had the habit of attacking any and everyone who questioned his authority. He went into this racial diatribe with the worker. And rudely refused to speak with her. He then demanded that a black worker be called. He wasn't going to talk to a "white devil". When he spoke like this, I've always found it ironic. His mother was white, so did that make him part white devil? So the lady obviously was shaken. She called the police, the notorious Henrico police. This police department was known for being the most racist in that part of the outskirts of Richmond. It was a relatively large Police Department and at that time I believe they had no more than two minority officers. If you were black driving in that area you would be stopped, no doubts about it. Whether you broke a traffic law or not. Even if you owned one of the many nice homes in that area. Quite a few blacks did live in this well-to-do area, but they pretty much went to work and back. There was no way they could cruise around on a Saturday night like a white resident could.

The "black" worker finally got there and he was nothing short of a black devil. He was completely rude, belligerent and downright hostile. My mother and I were trying to calm the situation down. But our attempts were overshadowed by Greg's ranting. My mom advised him to shut up but he didn't. By this time Greg called the black worker a uncle Tom. The police arrived and they separated each of us. After deliberation between the police and the workers, one of the workers approached us (by this time my mother and I were standing together) and let us know that they were going to remove the children. They informed us that it was only temporary and that a hearing before a judge would be held in three days time. I began to cry and asked that they not remove the children. I apologized on behalf of Greg's behavior. But to no avail, they had their minds made up. So they asked me to get the children together and I complied. By this time Greg and my mother were standing together outside of the hotel room. Greg told me not to cry. He said that I was empowering them with my tears. So I stopped crying for a short time, holding back my tears. My youngest child was only nine months old. He was not fully weaned. My second son and I had a strong bond that was ripped apart. Imagine the pain he must've felt. Being taken away from his mother who loved him and he loved back at just nine months old. I talked to him as I got him dressed, trying to calm him down. I vowed that he would be back with me in three days. Those three days turned into 15 months.

As if my life wasn't already shitty because of my mom's boyfriend, now he was the cause of my children being taken away from me. I was only guilty of being a good, loving, hard-working mother who would die for any of my children on a whim. By all means Greg was a monster but I knew that he wasn't physically or sexually abusing my children. After the children were all ready, CPS packed them into a minivan and left. Meanwhile the police were standing around outside the hotel room. My mom and her boyfriend got into the car and left, leaving me behind. The police went into the room and started looking through our belongings, throwing clothes around in the process. No, they didn't have a search warrant. Why did they do this, you may ask? Because they could. This is what it's like to be poor and black in this land. But more so poor, because I have witnessed the ill-treatment of poor whites as well.

I asked "What are you doing"? "You have no right to go through my stuff". They looked at me and chuckled. One of the officers responded by saying "If we can do this to Chuck Richardson then we can do it to you nigger". Chuck Richardson is a black Vietnam veteran turned City Councilman turned heroin addict. Mr.Richardson did two years in Henrico County jail because he wouldn't tell who he brought his heroin from.

Henrico County is also famous for taking custody of this lesbian woman's child some years ago. Sharon Bottoms was her name and her crime, being lesbian. Don't believe me? I'm pretty sure that you can Google these events and find more detailed information. As a matter of fact the lady's story made headline news nationwide.

Appalled, I asked for his badge number and name. I also told him that I would be filing a complaint against him. I let him know that I was going to tell his supervisors of the racial epithet he used against me. Another officer then said to me "You keep talking and we're going to lock you up" I respond by saying "You can't lock me up, I didn't break any law". Then a third officer says "That's it, turn around you're under arrest". "Under arrest, I didn't do anything". " What are you arresting me for"? I asked. "Trespassing" he said. "Trespassing, how can I be trespassing when I live here and the room is in my name"? "Tell it to the judge" he said. And let me tell you I was terrified. I had never been locked up or placed in handcuffs before. But not only that, when they took me outside, people were standing around looking at me. One of the people looking and laughing was actually a black lady who worked on the job with my mom and me. She also lived at this hotel. And ironically this black lady was a friend of my mom's in the late 70s. She actually held me and knew of me as a baby. I had never did anything to her, why would she laugh?

This particular cop that arrested me had this crazy accent. It sounded like a Rhode Island or Maine accent. Anyways he was very tall with dark hair and a olive complexion. But there was one thing off about him, he had blue eyes. Not to say that blue eyes are off but it was so mismatched on him. It didn't look natural. Eureka! I thought to myself, that's it, he's wearing blue contacts. So me being highly upset but knowing that it wouldn't be wise to curse out an officer. I said to him "Why are you doing this to me, no matter what you do you'll never be fully accepted". "Look at you, ashamed of your dark eyes so you go and wear blue contacts". Making direct eye contact with him I noticed that he was turning red. He then said "I got something special for you". He then went to the car and retrieved a pair of leg cuffs. As I'm standing outside for all eyes to see, he further humiliated me by putting leg cuffs on me. As you may know that wasn't protocol but who was I going to tell. And in that climate would justice really be served? I can look back at it now as just a learning experience and actually laugh. But at that moment I was afraid. I didn't know if he would take me off somewhere and beat me up or worse.

Thank God the jail wasn't a far distance from the hotel. He took me straight to jail,it may sound crazy but I was happy to be at the jail. I had rather been there then in some woods somewhere getting my ass beat with a blackjack. Yes, I was a 19-year-old woman but that never stopped violent racist before. Being a resident of Richmond, Virginia, you couldn't forget about racism. Everywhere you turned there was something to remind you of slavery. Everywhere you look, Confederate treasonous soldiers are being praised as heroes. In my opinion this should be against federal law, but that's another story.

Once at jail I was processed. The usual fingerprinting, personal information and mug shot. All new and embarrassing to me. They placed a bail on me. I don't recall exactly how much, but I was told by the bail bondsman later that night. That it was unusually high for trespassing especially being that I had never been in any kind of trouble before. He said that most people are just let go with a court summons.It turned out that my mom and her boyfriend had bailed me out. They told me that they paid $150 to get me out. And that was all the money they had. I'll admit I was happy to see them, I was not looking forward to going into population. We drove back to the hotel. My mom had the key to get into the room but it didn't work. We went to the office to resolve the problem. They informed us that we were no longer welcomed on the property. So the manager escorted us to the room to remove our belongings. After packing the car, Greg told my mom to go to the office and get the refund. We had just paid for a full week one day prior. That would have been decent money, minus 1 day stay. Get this, they flatly refused to give the refund. The manager who was there when the police were dispatched earlier, said that they were keeping our money because the police were called. And that if we didn't hurry up and leave, he would call the police and have all three of us arrested. It was a losing battle. The most we could do was sue in civil court. Which would have taken time and more money that we didn't have. So we quietly walked away. I guess they all ate at Denny's that night! My mother was estranged from her family and Greg didn't want his family to know what we were going through (they had a tendency to gossip, a lot) they decided that we were to sleep in the car. We slept in the car for about a week. And it was miserable. Bathing in the service stations each a.m. Then going to work still tired and sore from basically sleeping while sitting up each night. We ate free food from our job and told no one about the situation. My mom's boyfriend had some jewelry that he pawned for gas money. That one week felt like two weeks. Late at night Greg would drive us to a local park that had free water. We would fill up jugs of water and shower in the dark of the night after the park was closed.

When we went to Family Court I was so sure that I would be get my children back that same day. But after the workers and police testified that they didn't feel the children would be safe being returned home just yet, my hopes were crushed. We at that time weren't represented by a attorney nor were we allowed to testify on our own behalf. But honestly I don't think it would have made a difference. They informed the judge that we were homeless and we would have to at least get permanent housing before the children could come back. My mother and I got paid from our jobs about a week after the children were taken. We took some of our pay and rented a hotel room. After that one week, Greg decided to ask one of his aunts if we could stay with her for a while. There was no way we could save for an apartment paying $200 a week plus the car note, auto insurance and food. She allowed us to stay there and he agreed to pay her $75 per week. A lot for a widow who already had a comfortable life. My mom's boyfriend decided that my mother and I had to find better paying jobs. We were killing ourselves working two fast food jobs and not receiving much pay.

In Richmond there are not many well-paying jobs. And I've had many jobs. I've been a waitress, maid, car wash girl, cashier, cook, prep chef, hostess and thief (only to feed my family). So Greg decided that my mother and I should apply at Tysons chicken processing plant. That was the next best paying job outside of Philip Morris or DuPont. Those jobs were like gold. The starting wages were like $14 an hour. You had to know somebody to get in and they mostly hired family. Those jobs people didn't quit, they retired. My mom and I both applied at Tyson. We were called back within days. They notified us that we had to pass a physical and a background check. That was no problem. We started working the next day after taking the drug test. We were hired for the third shift in the sanitation department. Our responsibilities included cleaning the machines that cut the processed chicken into parts. We also had to be very thorough in our jobs as the USDA inspected each machine every a.m. We started our shift at 12 o'clock midnight and got off at roughly 6:00 AM. But we were paid for eight hours. These hours worked for us as me and my mother were going to court frequently to get our babies back. My job there entailed cleaning a machine that de-boned chicken breasts. The badder machine it was called. A very challenging machine. Funny thing is, that this particular machine was previously assigned to men only. It required much bending, lifting and climbing all while holding a high-pressure hose. My supervisor kept me on the machine as I never got any write-ups from the USDA. Something that was frequent before I started working there. The only drawbacks from this job was the smell of wet chicken fat as well as being soaked. We were supplied a rain suit but that couldn't keep out all the water. Working there I didn't make many friends. A few older ladies and men spoke to me when they get off from work on the second shift. There were Cambodian and Mexican people working there as well. I befriended some Cambodian girls who I would casually chat with sometimes. There was one black Vietnamese girl who started working there. I felt so sorry for her because all the other Asian girls there were Cambodian. Anyone who knows a little about South East Asian history knows that Vietnamese and Cambodians generally don't get along due to their past political conflicts.

Once I was sitting on the bench in the hallway taking a little break. She saw me and asked me something in Vietnamese. Now I don't know anything about the language but I assumed she was asking me if I was from Vietnam. She and I looked a lot alike. So I responded back to her in English saying "Am

I from Vietnam"? She nodded her head with a smile anticipating that I was. I then shook my head and said "no". She then walked away with the saddest look on her face.

Personally I've always empathized with immigrants and foreigners. Even though I am American by blood and nationality, I've always felt like an outsider. I never fit in but foreigners seemed to accept me. I was constantly rejected by my own. Blacks have always treated me like I wasn't one of them, though by all means I am.

Working there I came into contact with many men. And many of them would try to hit on me. I totally rebuffed each and every one of them. My excuse was that I already had a boyfriend. I desired to be like any other girl my age. To like a guy, go on dates, go steady, fall in love, get married. You know the whole nine but I knew that could never happen as long as I was in that situation. So I didn't bother playing or flirting back. My mother loved drama. And more than drama she loved to report to him if I spoke or smiled at any guy. Whether he was blind, crippled or crazy. So to counter this, I would tell of every guy who looked, smiled or spoke to me. Being sure to be a obedient girl as I didn't want to suffer from the torture and blows my mom suffered often.

I recall once this black guy tried to talk to me. He gave me compliments about my looks and I thanked him. He then asked if he could be my boyfriend. He went through this drawn out monologue about how he would take care of me, treat me good and do anything for me. I politely told him "Sorry, but I already have somebody, if I didn't I would be your girl". He then looked at me and said "You just think you all that cause you light skinned" Baffled I looked around. Who was he calling light-skinned? I've never viewed myself as light-skinned. I laughed in his face, I couldn't hold it in. I responded by saying "Who me, light-skinned? I'm not light-skinned and I don't think that I'm better than anyone darker than me". He walked away showing obvious disappointment but I let him down as softly as I could.

In the midst of us working this new job we had to go to Family Court. Each time there was something different. A different concern that the guardian ad lightum and prosecutor wanted addressed. First, we had to find permanent housing. Then extensive drug screens, next psychological testing to ensure that we weren't deranged.

And then the rumor mill started. Apparently they talked to each of our extended family members. And they told them that they believed he was the father of my children. So that became a big issue. The age of consent in Virginia at the time was 16 I believe. I gave birth to my first child at 14 and my second at 15. My first thought was okay finally I can tell someone and have justice. But then Satan (his well-deserved nickname I gave him) got into my ear and told me that I had better not tell on him. He told me that if I told, they would lock him up for very long time, lock my mother up for very long time, place my siblings up for adoption, deem me mentally unstable and unfit as a parent, take away my children and place them up for adoption. He said that if I betrayed him no one would win. Sadly, I believed him. In my opinion they hadn't played fair from day one. The police officer called me a nigger, locked me up without just cause, placed a very high bond on me, dragged me into this drama as if I had did something wrong. In my opinion they should have dealt solely with him. So after assessing the facts, I decided to cover for him. I'll get away from him someday but this is not the best way out. My mom treated me like pure shit. I recall when I first told her that he was sodomizing me. She calmly said "Won't you tell your counselors at school"? "But mom if I do they're just going to lock him up and if he gets locked up someone might kill him in jail and then it would be my fault" I replied. She then replied "Well you gotta tell somebody because he ain't right". Later that night as if my prayers had been answered, he and my mom got into an argument. He believed that my newborn brother wasn't his son. So he packed his belongings and decided to go move back in with his grandmother. Just as he was about to cross the threshold my mother said "If you leave me I'm going to the police and tell them that you been fucking my daughter". He stopped in his tracks right then, turned around and walked directly to me. He looked me directly in my eyes as if he wanted to rip me apart with his bare hands. And he said "You told her some shit like that". Out of fear I initially denied saying it. After he asked me again, I then admitted to telling her. But I back-pedaled and looked at my mother and said "Mom I lied, he didn't do that. I just said that to make you guys break up". He then looked at me and said "Where did you get that from"? I said that I had read it in the newspaper. My mother's tactic worked, he didn't leave her that night and still hasn't. At that moment I felt betrayed to the highest level. I hated my mother for many years after that. She knew what I told her was absolute truth but she didn't care, all she wanted was him in her life. Whatever the cost, even the brutal rapes of her oldest daughter. She cared nothing about my mental or physical well-being. I was only her token. Only there for his and her disposal. She hated me but I still found within my heart a small amount of love and loyalty towards her. So at that time I couldn't stomach being the cause of my mother being locked away.

So month after month they asked and interviewed me. But I vehemently denied it. I made up a name of some boy and said that I didn't know where he currently was. I told them that he was Jamaican and that he may have went back to his country. So while going through that battle I had yet another to fight. I had to go to court on the fabricated trespassing charge. I couldn't afford a lawyer so one was appointed to me. In Virginia court appointed doesn't spell out crappy lawyer. In that state even the most talented, well-paid lawyers must volunteer for X amount of hours per month pro bono. I was the most fortunate. The lawyer that was chosen for me, was a lawyer from Michael Morrissey law firm. His name too was Greg, I forgot his last name.

Now Michael Morrissey was one of the most talented lawyers in the South East. And he only hired gifted lawyers who were like-minded. Michael Morrissey started as a very talented prosecutor. His conviction rate was 100% or darn close. He could make Santa Claus look like a cat burglar and mother Theresa look like a slut.But later in his career he chose to become a defense attorney. Michael Morrissey was so passionate about defending people that on numerous occasions he would raised his monotone in court. And has been known to even snap on the judge or prosecutor if he felt that his client wasn't being treated fairly. He had even been threatened to be disbarred quite a few times. Not that he was an irrational hothead but his style of practicing law wasn't appreciated in the ultra-conservative, ultra racist, good old boy fashion of Virginia. Last I checked he is now a general assemblyman in Richmond.

Anyway when I went to meet with Greg (the lawyer) let me tell you, I looked horrible. I looked like hammered shit! My hair was unkempt, I had on a baseball cap turned to the back in a attempt to disguise it. I had on a pair of my mom's boyfriend baggie jean shorts, one of his oversized T-shirts and some old dirty sneakers. Not only did I look unlady like, but I felt unladylike. If you could have saw me, your first impression probably would have been that I was a young Butch lesbian. Honestly that's what I looked like, sat like and talked like. I only met with this lawyer once but I told him everything that was done and said in verbatim. He didn't act surprised about the nigger thing. He did seem to believe me. He also asked had I ever been in trouble before. I let him know that I hadn't. He then explained to me some laws pertaining to trespassing. He also let me know that I shouldn't worry so much because trespassing wasn't a big charge and based on numerous factors worst-case scenario would be a fine, but no jail time. He advised me to plead not guilty based on the information I gave him. He advised me to dress nicely when I came to court. Embarrassing right? My lawyer asked me to basically look presentable on the court date! So as the court date approached I was able to groom myself to look more presentable.

I've always taken pride in my overall appearance. That was the only outlet I had for many years. I had to stay in the house when not working and I became bored rather easily. So out of boredom I would brush my hair, groom my brows and paint my nails. So on the court date, I got to court about 30 minutes before docket as my lawyer had instructed me to. I made direct eye contact with him and he said nothing. So I noticed him looking around for someone. I assumed that he was looking for me, so I called his name. He looked at me with bewilderment. Showing signs of being flabbergasted as I told him my name and let him know that I was his client. Stunned he said "You're Shakira". I had completely transformed myself into a new creature, I assume a pretty one. So guys you can't always judge a book by its cover. I'm sure he had me sized up as some smart mouth, hardened girl who wanted to be a boy but that was the furthest from who I am. We went into the courtroom and I was called not long after being seated. The cop didn't show up, ironically something else came up on the day of the trial. The judge whose name I can't remember, was utterly nasty to me. I was already being victimized by basically being dragged into court when I was completely innocent. But then the judge acted as if he had something against me. I could only think of one thing, my skin color. He went into this speech about how he didn't want to see me in his courtroom again. And that "You had better not be on their property ever again" he also told me that "You have been warned, if you're caught on their property again I will lock you up". I calmly stood there and said "Yes, your honor". The whole process took about ten minutes. The case was dismissed.

Meanwhile on the other front-line, we were scheduled for our evaluations and drug tests. We complied and passed both. Next we had to find permanent housing. My mom found an apartment in the West end and put it in my name. Okay I thought my children will be back with me any moment now. No, the prosecutors kept pushing for the DNA test. After months of an uphill battle, the judge finally said that he wasn't going to order DNA test. This judge was about to retire. So on our next hearing we had a new judge, a female. Now this woman had issues. She would obviously be intoxicated, slurred and for-getful. It's funny how having a degree and title make some people oblivious. But even a deaf, blind man could hear and see that she was heavily influenced by alcohol. Yet no one, none of these highly educated, intelligent, fighters of justice dared to say anything. Here was a person judging me yet didn't have the discipline to drink after work. And mind you the hearings would start no later than 10:00 AM.

Next we were told that we had to get to separate apartments since we didn't take the DNA tests. That was the only way CPS would feel comfortable letting the children come back. So my mom and I started working doubles to save up money for yet another apartment. My mother and her boyfriend got a apart-ment in Church Hill. Where she,Greg and their children were to live. On one of the hearings the judge had ordered me to have furniture, water, electric and gas within 30 days time. Will within 30 days, I could only afford to get the elec-tric on. I was making only about $250 per week and I was working very hard for that. My apartment costs $325 per month. The realtors required one month in advance deposit, a total of $650. My electric, gas and water required deposits as I had never had any of these utilities before. All I needed was a little help, even with my pride I still would have taken it to get my children back sooner. But no such programs exists in one of the nations most wealthiest states. In Virginia, CPS or welfare for that matter don't assist you with utilities, furniture etc. You must go to a church to get help, if they don't have the resources, oh well! And if you had a job then you couldn't even receive food stamps at that time. Is like you're being set up to be some welfare receiving louse. If you try to better your-self by attempting to climb the ladder then the fine lawmakers of Virginia are all too happy to remove the next step of the ladder.

So when I returned to court the judge asked me "Did you do everything that was ordered"? I explained to her that I managed to get the electric on but wasn't able to get everything else done because I didn't have the money. After my testimony she gave some little speech and I don't remember exactly what was said. But I know that I was shocked when she said that she was going to find me in contempt of court. And I was even more flabbergasted when she said that I was to serve 30 days in jail. 10 days for each contempt. Even though I heard and understood what she said, I couldn't wrap my mind around being locked away for 30 days because I couldn't afford to get all of my utilities on. I asked my then lawyer to translate what she said as if she spoke a foreign language. If I could see the look on my face in present time, I'm sure that I would laugh at myself.

My dilemma was purely financial and by no means did I mean to be disrespectful to the judge, the courts or my children. This miscarriage of justice against me only made me lose any small amount of trust I had of the system since my pseudo-trespassing charge. This only reaffirmed in my mind that I had made the right choice by not telling of the horrors I experienced growing up under the guise of my mom and her boyfriend. If you ever played the board game Monopoly, it was like that for me. You know when you get that go directly to jail card. Except this was real! Yep they took me directly to jail. The jail was connected to the court, so the court bailiff escorted me there. Here we go again! The fingerprinting, the mug shot, the strip searching and that horrible smelling County jail jumpsuit. Now I have never smelled burning flesh but I could imagine that this is what it smells like. I've always wondered if they added some kind of detergent that had been chemically engineered to be funky as a part of the punishment. I was so afraid because this time there was no bail to be posted, no chance of me staying in the holding pin by myself as before. And to make matters worse this time it was for 30 days. 30 days in population around junkies, prostitutes, bullies etc. For the life of me I couldn't understand why? Why would she lock me up for 30 days? Knowing very well that I had a job and apartment to maintain. And that meager pay from this job was the only way I was going to get my babies back. Thank goodness that I had a rapport with my supervisor, Gladys.

Gladys was a short, tough black lady from Mississippi. Her speech pattern was so fast that at times it was hard to understand her, coupled with her heavy southern drawl. Anyways she had given my mom and I her home phone number just in case something came up. We had already given her a brief background on our Family Court situation. So when I called her collect and explained to her where I was, she was very understanding. She assured me that my job would still be available when I got out. I was one of her top workers and it paid off when I needed it most. Being a late teen and incarcerated amongst older women from all walks of life, was a completely new experience for me. I'll admit that I was fearful. Not that I was a particularly shaky person but I wondered would being in those surroundings force me to become someone I'm not? Will I have to fight, curse and go for bad to make it for 30 days? Will these women try to attack my street credibility? Will they think they can take advantage of me because I was there for contempt of court? These are the questions that came to my mind. I'm sure that everyone has had similar questions the first time being incarcerated. And I'm sure that men are plagued with many more questions. I decided that I would woman up. There was nothing immediate that could be done to get me out of there.

So when I was taken to population, I held my head high, made direct eye contact and didn't smile. I told myself that if any girl attempts to fight me, I'll fight back with all my heart. (A lesson learned from my middle school days, where I once fought a bully twice as big as me) No matter how much bigger or older than me the girl was. Surprisingly none of the women were mean to me. I was bunked with a 18-year-old black girl who was arrested for shoplifting and a Apache-Italian lady in her late 20s, who was arrested for DUI. We talked well into the night, each of them telling a little about their life. I told a very little of mine and never got too personal. After about three days the 18-year-old was released, having served her time. And the Apache' lady was switched into another day room with women her age who were also substance abusers. I next was paired with a black woman who was the mother of three. I didn't ask her age but she appeared to be in her late 20s. According to her she was arrested for shoplifting due to her drug habit. She said that she use to be addicted to heroin. She then kicked that drug and got hooked on methadone. I let her know that I was locked up for contempt of court. But of course I dramatized it some. I told her that I started fussing in court and that's why I was charged with contempt. Making it melodramatic was my way of saving face. I mean how could I tell any of the inmates that I was locked away for basically nothing. And that I wasn't detained in blazing glory but in fact was very peaceful and cooperative. The lady that I bunked with had a lot of money on her canteen. The jailhouse commissary was called the canteen. The way it works is a family member or friend would put money on your books (something like a small escrow account). You in return are credited with the dollar for dollar amount. With this credit you can purchase all sorts of junk food, skin care products, hair care products etc. All approved by the warden as being safe products. Some of the girls would buy packs of cherry Kool-Aid and Vaseline. They mixed the two together and walla you had jailhouse lip gloss. So anyway my bunk partner must have noticed that I didn't have any canteen.One reason being that I couldn't receive canteen until I had been classified. And up to that point I hadn't been. So she offered me one of her many packs of hostess chocolate cupcakes. Now I had never been locked up for any stretch of time before but even I know that you don't accept any food etc. from anyone in prison or jail. That's the persons way of trying to make you their flunky or worse.These rules apply for any inmate,whether male or female. Remember that no fellow inmate gives a damn about you that much. Because having someone on the outside who cares for you that much is hard to come by. Taking favors in jail is serious business.

So needless to say I declined. She asked me again this time smiling and using a softer voice. I declined again this time not smiling and used a firmer voice. She said okay and then dropped that scheme. When the others would go outside or to some kind of meeting, I stayed in the cell by myself. I actually read some novel that was lying around in the day room. It took me three days to read. Now for me that was a great feat. I'm a Gemini for goodness sake and anyone who knows Gemini knows that we seldom read a book from front to back. I read this one book out of sheer boredom. I can't even recall the author, title or storyline. So after about six or seven days, Greg came up with the bright idea that I should appeal the judge's decision. So I contacted my attorney directly and let him know that I wanted to appeal. By appealing I would be released without bond. There was no bond for contempt of court and through the appellant process, I was considered innocent until my case was heard by a higher judge. So on the ninth day, the day I was to be classified. And placed in population with the more rowdy girls my age, I was released thank God. I tell you, those nine days felt like at least two weeks. Time moved slow in jail. I had a new hearing shortly and the judge dropped the remaining days saying that my time was served. Truth be told, I was told by a very knowledgeable source that the maximum for contempt was 10 days, not 30. What a blunder of justice! If it wasn't for Greg at that time I would have just did the 30 days, though unjust. It was things like this that at times made me think through all his evilness he must love me, somewhat. Reflecting now, I believe that it was for his own protection. He must have figured that 30 days away from him I would surely break and tell someone of the horrors committed against me. And I'm sure there were plenty of jailhouse informants.

I went back to work the same day I was released and my supervisor expressed how happy she was to see me. Telling me how the machine had been written up when I was away. Being back on the grind, Greg made sure that I did over time to make up for the money he missed while I was locked up. Honestly I did not mind though, the more time out of the house and away from him the better. It's funny how people sometimes use work as a way to escape their problems at home. I myself am guilty of this. I didn't get everything in order until maybe 1 1/2 months later. The hearings were scheduled on a monthly basis. So the first month after being released I was prepared to once again be arrested as I didn't complete everything. But thank God I wasn't. The hearing after that everything was completed. Now I was told that I had to comply with in-home counseling to allow time for my children to transition back to me, their mother. Truth be told, I was so sick of hearing the word transition. No one cared to "transition" them away from me. They just abruptly took them. My nine month old, my five-year-old and my three-year-old. Something I never understood was, there was a lady who lived next door to us at the hotel. She was addicted to crack and had two sons and a little girl around five or six. I would personally see old white guys come to the hotel room and she and her sons would step outside while the little girl was inside. I can only imagine what was going on. They moved away and I found out a short time later why. It turned out that CPS took her children away. I felt so sorry for the little girl. I had a strong feeling of what she was going through but felt powerless to help. I felt powerless to help myself. The real ass kicker here for me is that she got her children back several months before I got mine back. She had a quick plan. Move Into the projects, get a fast food job, go to rehab for several months and get her children back. Anyway we started receiving in-home counseling. The counselors were okay by me but my mom's boyfriend had a problem with them. He had problems with every body. When they would come over to my apartment sometimes my mother and her boyfriend would be seen. Other times they would be there but not seen. They were always afraid to let me out of their sight for too long. They would always tell me that they acted like this for my protection, sadly at that time I believed them. I recall several occasions Greg telling me that Patty, I'll call the female counselor and Brian, I'll call the male counselor, told him that I was slow. Meaning mentally challenged. And that they would only fully recommend the children be returned if they were assured that my mom and her boyfriend were always around to help me. I don't know if I ever appeared withdrawn to them but if I did it was only because prior to the visit Greg would give me the business about how they didn't like me and how they couldn't be trusted. Older and wiser now, I believe that these so-called comments of me being considered mentally challenged were wholly fabricated by Greg. As a means of further control and manipulation. After the visit if I were too friendly, Greg would accuse me of sleeping with Brian. I tell you he was unrelenting in his psychological warfare against me.

Long story short we got our children back. I was honestly happy that the judge ordered us to live separately. I was hoping that this was my chance to get away. But my mom's boyfriend,Greg, wouldn't have it. I would lie in bed at night and wonder if I could maintain without them around.But self-doubt and reality set in. I made about $1000 a month before taxes. My job was out of city limits which meant I had to take a car to get out there. I couldn't afford a car, I couldn't drive nor had a license. My oldest was about to start school so I needed someone to take her to school as I got off from work at 6 am. I then would need a babysitter for my other two children which meant more expenses. And I'm not talking about paying rent, utilities, food, doctors bills and clothes. All while working my ass off just to make under thousand dollars a month. I had no other family that I was on good terms with. I was convinced that my father was scum and I partially blamed him for my living in hell. So what was I to do, where was I to go?

Being from the South,I got use to thinking of being completely self-sufficient. Because the government there doesn't help the needy much. I knew that even if I told what was happening to me than there still would be no real help. No,I told myself, now is not the time but one day.

Back to business as usual, my mom and I worked hard to keep Greg with nice cars and feed his materialism.He brought himself (funded through us) gold bracelets, necklaces and rings. Claiming that the world was going to end any day now and that gold was the only currency to be accepted at that time. I brought his bullshit for many years. You know the doomsday BS, the Antichrist BS. Us believers, us Christians had to fight and flee if we didn't want to be beheaded. My mom's boyfriend always assured me that I was in good hands. He knew how to shoot weapons, military strategies, and how to survive off the land, so he said. In a twisted way I felt happy that he was in my life to protect me from "the beast" if nothing else. How absurd? The monster who abused my mother, raped and sodomized me since I was a young child, beat and enslaved me, protect me? I believed whole heartedly in revelations of the New Testament. I read it from front to back so many times to figure out the riddles of the "word". I had been bred as a little girl to be fearful of the world, fearful of this beast with seven heads, 10 crowns etc. Not seeing that the true beast or beasts were right under my roof, posing as my parents.

When my mom and I received our w-2 forms he got really excited. That was a time when he could really do big things for his self. Not long after the children came back and not long before we moved from Virginia, he decided that he wanted a red sports car. A red Dodge stealth. It was beautiful and everything but that was the only car we had. He vowed to purchase a van of some sort to transport the family. Instead he took all of our refund money somewhere in the neighborhood of $5000 and put it all on this car. Leaving us stuck with a 300+ dollar a month car note and expensive auto insurance to pay. We were nothing but his slaves in a pure sense of the word. Now be reminded that at this time I had three children and my mother had three children. That alone totals six children add the adults and that was nine people. Nine people and he decided to get a sports car.

No matter the hardships he went through, he was always the same old devil. It was somewhat of an routine to take us to work on time and pick us up late most days, except payday. On payday he never picked us up late. One night on the way to work, he and my mother had been drinking. And when my mother drank she got loud, reckless and very verbal, not in a good way! So she started nothing short of cursing him out for picking us up late. " Motherfucker this, motherfucker that, bitch this, bitch that". He told my mom "Keep talking shit and I ain't gonna pick you up tomorrow morning" So she went on blabbing. So out of fear for her, I said "Mom can you just be quiet". She got quiet and I calmly said that "All momma is trying to say, is that it's not right to pick us up late almost every day. When we get off we're really tired". He then said "That's all she had to say, she ain't have to talk all that other shit". Things calmed down. My mom got out of the passenger seat, I got out of the backseat and we said "See you later" to him and went into work. Six hours later we're off from work and we went outside. He was nowhere to be found. I didn't panic too much, I thought he was just going to be late again today. Minutes turned into tens of minutes, tens of minutes turned its hours. Now at other times if he were that late, our supervisor, Gladys, would give us a ride home. But today she had to stay back even later for some management meeting. It was now about 9:30 AM and we had gotten off at 6:00 AM. We had no cell phone or house phone. The only communication at that time was a pager. He had the pager and my mother spent what little change she had paging him numerous times. There was no one else we trusted, no family we could call and no money. So we had to go with our only option, we walked home. My mom and I walked a total of 17 miles from rural Glen Allen, Virginia to the Richmond city limits.

Two women walking on the side of a rural highway. We could have been hit by a car, kidnapped,raped, bitten by one of the many coral snakes that were out there or anything. We finally got home a little after 1 PM to find him knocked out on the sofa. We banged on the door because we weren't allowed to have keys. He woke up, opened the door and went back to lie down. I calmly said "How could you do that to us, we had to walk home"? He replied "Fuck you bitch, I told you I won't coming to pick you up ho". He told my mom that he wasn't coming to pick her up if she kept talking. But she got quiet after that, and exited the car on quasi-good terms. To make the situation harsher, I was about two or three weeks pregnant with my third son. Although I didn't find out I was pregnant for certain until a few weeks later.

My mother had to walk to pick up the children from school and the baby-sitter. We also had to help the children with their homework,bathe them, cook dinner, feed them and put them to bed all while trying to get rest for work. We had to be to work again that night. In order to get there on time we left the house each night at 11:00 PM. I had blood clots on the bottom of my feet and my mom had blisters on hers. My mother several days later told me that he told her he went out with his younger stepsister and smoked weed laced with heroin. And that he really was too out of it to pick us up. He's a liar, my mom's a liar so even now I don't know what to believe but I know what was said to me and that he didn't pick us up. As anyone could have predicted, we were unable to keep this precious car. It was okay for drive to him, but he hated paying bills. To the tune of $700 per month alone didn't make it more appealing. All of the money I worked so hard for had just gone down the drain. Money-wise that was nothing compared to what he would do in the future. He brought a minivan finally and we eventually ended up living back in a motel.

Later in my pregnancy I was actually forced onto maternity leave. At the time I was pretty pissed at my supervisor because when I made her aware of my pregnancy within the first trimester. She said that she would give me light-duty when I got further along. The problem was that in Virginia you don't receive any kind of assistance when you go on maternity leave. And no one else would hire a 7 1/2 half month pregnant woman. So if you don't have at least a few grand saved or a husband with a good income, you're pretty screwed. Unless of course I decided to apply for welfare. Which it self was a long process and a major headache, with the benefits not being so great.Plus they were really strict with the paternity thing and I hated being dishonest about who my children's father is. Being that we were now living in a motel, the rent was due a weekly basis. This forced my mom's boyfriend to get a job. Something he should have done all the long.But he did this under one condition, my mom had to work with him. He was always paranoid that someone wanted to kill him. So she would be there to watch his back if you will. He decided that it would be better for my mom to quit the chicken processing plant. So after two years of working there that's exactly what she did. However she worked two jobs. One job was a doughnut shop up the street from where we lived. The other was at a drive-through burger joint where they worked together. When I was pregnant he wasn't as mean to me. He made sure I ate well and didn't argue with me as much. But he still had his ways. While they were at work, I would stay in the motel room watching baby stories (a show about pregnant women preparing to have their babies) longing to be normal. Here I was pregnant for the fourth time by an abusive, rapist, living in a motel room with no money, no job, no education and no one I could count on.

My sons kicks inside my womb were like air to the earth, much-needed. In my mind, it was his special way of saying "Keep going mom, I need you, stay strong". And I heard him loud and clear. On the burger job there was some Indian girl who befriended them. She was moving to Philadelphia with her boyfriend. From what I was told she really hated Virginia. She was originally from a third world country and hated Virginia. What does that say about that place. Long story short she advised them to move out of Virginia. She said that there were so much more opportunities in the North East. Greg came home one day and said that when we got out tax return money, we were moving to New Jersey, his birth state. I asked could I wait until the baby was born. It was some time in December and my son was due to be born on February 2nd. He agreed and vowed that when we moved to New Jersey, he was going to be a better person. Be supportive, contribute more financially, help me get my own apartment, car and license. Yada yada yada, the same bullshit heard it all before. Something you must understand is that he is the most convincing, cold, callous and manipulative liar. He would say any and every thing to get his way and once he got what he wanted he turned on you like a cobra. Sticking his fangs into your juggler making you regret your naivety with every bite. I've said all that to say that I believed him. I guess that's what your mind does when you've been trapped. Acknowledging that you have no way out only makes you feel worst.

My third son was born on February 3rd. He was a healthy 8 lbs. 13 oz. baby. Beautiful, strong and feisty even as a newborn. With this child I had to undergo a emergency C-section. Because I didn't dilate enough even after large doses of Pitocin. So after four days in hospital, my son and I were released with a clean bill of health, thank God. A few days later we were on the road heading to New Jersey. When we first arrived in Camden, it was a culture shock for me. Yes, we have ghettos in the South. Yes, I've lived as some of the worst ghettos. Yes, in the ghetto people generally put bars on their windows. But I had never saw a front porch enclosed with bars. Greg decided that we should go to Atlantic city to try and gain employment with one of the casinos. So from Camden he drove to Atlantic City. There we got a hotel room with two king sized beds. Normally I would sleep on the floor, making a pallet with thick blankets. But because of the C-section I was allowed to sleep on one of the beds with my youngest children. Greg and my mom shared the other bed. The oldest children made pallets. After moving expenses we still had around $2000. My mom's boyfriend had the bright idea to go and gamble. My mother and I hadn't found jobs at that point. We had applied at a few casinos but that was a very long process. Just filling out the application was frustrating. We had to fill out a 15 to 20 page thick application and attach a recent photo with the casino commission.We returned all applications and waited for a call back.

So when Greg went to gamble I stayed in the hotel with the children. My mom went with him. The first night he went he came back a short time later and announced that he had won $500. He then ordered take-out pizza for the children and take-out Chinese for the adults. The next night he decided to go back again but this time he stayed for a longer period. He and my mother came back several hours later. He looked completely haggard. His clothes were disheveled, he reeked of cigarettes and alcohol. He had this look of panic on his face. Seeing this, I asked him what was wrong. He then informed me that he had lost all of the money gambling. I then said "But you have the rent money right". He responded "Nope" I immediately started crying. He then told me to stop crying. He said that he'd figure something out. He then informed me that he and my mom had checks down south. They were paid biweekly and their pay date had just come up. I then said "But those checks are down south and the rent is due tomorrow" He then said "Don't worry I'll go talk to the Indian guy" (the manager of the hotel). So he and my mom went downstairs to speak with management. They came back a short time later.Greg told me "Don't worry I got everything straight, the Indian guy even gave me gas money to get there. Yall don't have nothing to worry about". "He said that he's not going to put us out, he'll give us until tomorrow night to pay the rent". I was very relieved to hear that. And thank God that we already had food. He and my mother left for Virginia a short time later. After they left I started to feel uneasy again. Asking myself, What if the manager changes his mind or forgets their agreement? What if they get into a car accident or get hurt some other way? What if they never come back? I began to pray that those questions left my mind but they remained.Needless to say, I didn't get very much sleep that night.

Now in my current state of mind, being free from bondage. In retrospect, I wonder what secrets have they hidden from me? Most if not all of what they have ever told me have been lies. Those two have a wicked bond like I thought I would never witness.

They returned the following evening with their checks cashed and rent paid for that week. They still had several hundred dollars remaining. I believe it was somewhere around $300-$400. Again he went to gamble. And again he lost the money but this time he came back not the least bit humble. Instead he told my mom and I that we had to get a job ,quick. No more waiting for callbacks but we had to get a fast food job where we could be hired on the spot. And this is what we did. Early the following a.m., my mom and I went to apply at the local McDonald's. For me this was a great feat as I was about 2 1/2 weeks out of major surgery. My C-section incision was not fully healed. But I pushed through the pain because I knew that he wasn't going to work. And I had to take care of my children. We were hired that same morning. We were told to start that following a.m. By this time my mom had gotten a referral for the food bank to get food. We had so much canned meat, soup and veggies that food wasn't a concern. At the end of the week, rent was due and we didn't have it. So we were forced to sleep in the minivan. Imagine having a three-week old newborn, three small children, working at a fast food place, having to wash up at service stations. Eating canned food, wrapping up in blankets to stay warm through the night. Thank God we had to endure that for only about a week.

He at that time was receiving SSI so his payment was received about a week later. He then decided to venture off into another area south jersey. So our next stop was Burlington County. We got a rank dank motel room in Cinnaminson. There was an ice cream cone factory in Pennsauken that me and my mom started working. Greg also started working there. But it didn't take long before he started to complain.So all three of us quit.

While living in Cinnaminson we met this older woman who took a liking to my mother. She herself had migrated from North Carolina some 30 years ago. Her name was Vivian, may she rest in peace, she was a kind soul.

We moved from motel into another as we could never stay at any motel for long. Management would say that there were too many people in one room and we certainly couldn't afford to pay for two rooms. Another motel, another job. I don't recall any significant stability in my childhood or early adulthood. My mother and I went to a temporary service where they sent us to work in a factory that made medical wires. So in the midst of working I would take time to school my children. I've always wanted them to be enrolled in school. Where I felt the teaching format would be better and they could assimilate into society easier as adults. I've always wanted the best for my children. But their father saw it differently. He didn't want them in school. He was always pessimistic about the future. Pessimistic about anyone's hopes, dreams or aspirations that wouldn't include him. And at that time I was powerless and he made sure that I stayed aware of it.

At this new job I was required, as with all other jobs, to report to him everything that was said to me. I was also required to report anything that was said to my mother. Likewise she was required to report anything that was said to me. There were times when a male coworker would say something to me. And like a obedient slave I would go and tell Greg everything that was said in verbatim. The accusations would start and my mother would call me a fool behind his back saying that I shouldn't tell him everything. But I recalled the days of her not "telling everything" and what he would do to her. Not to mention that if I didn't tell my mom would have. Except in her version, there would have been so much exaggeration. It would have been much more colorful. My so-called mother had done this to me so many times.

At this point though it was mostly verbal abuse. He still hit my mom periodically, but not as frequent. I declare my mom developed a liking to being abused. She would have the most pleased look on her face after receiving a black eye. I recall once while we were working on this job. He stomped her ankle so badly that it swelled about twice its normal size. She hopped on that ankle for like three weeks straight. Telling her coworkers that she sprained her ankle. It took so long to heal, I wonder was it indeed fractured. Rumors began spreading that the company was going to close down its Cherry Hill location and move back to California. Hearing this we thought it would be best to have another job as we couldn't afford to be unemployed for one day. We were still paying rent on a week to week basis. So her and I started job hunting and found a book warehouse in Moorestown. We worked third shift there. I really enjoyed this job. It allowed me to be exposed to so many books. I couldn't read but so much though, after all I was there to ship books not read them. But when ever I could read the back cover I did and it made me happy. So it wasn't long before the rumors on the other job came to pass and us temporary employees were the first to go. Around this time he would cook for us. Make sure our clothes were clean, the children's clothes were clean,fed and educated. He seemed to be changing for the better, if that is at all possible. He even appeared to love our children. He would spend time with the boys, play with them and teach them guy stuff. I recall him holding our newborn son for hours as he and the boys watched boxing.

My mom and I shortly started working two jobs again. The second job was at a frozen food company in Pennsauken. We had the glorious task of boxing a South Jersey treat, soft pretzels. After about the third day the night supervisor made it evident that he didn't like me. He would complain that I wasn't boxing them fast enough. Now I have always been a efficient worker, so this claim was a copout. Honestly I think he didn't like my demeanor. We worked around mostly immigrants and undereducated people. I guess I conducted myself in a way that appalled him. I let it be known that I knew we were equals. It's people like him that made me reminisce about when I was working at a fast food restaurant down south. And this old lady entered the restaurant with a cargo van full of children. Evidently she was a driver for a after-school program. I asked to take her order and she went right into this rant. Saying to me "How dare you speak to me girl, what is your problem. You hold your head down when you talk to me, you don't look me in my eyes". "Who do you think you are"? It was 1997 and she still seemed to believe it was the 50s or something. I couldn't make this up. I stayed calm and took the children's orders. The nicer I was to her the angrier she got but it was no sweat on my back. And yes I continued to make eye contact with her with a smile on my face. I pitied her for being stuck in the Jim Crow days and not being able to accept diversity. If she could see that we currently have a president of black African descent, I'm sure she would roll over in her grave. She was very old back then so I'm sure she has since kicked the bucket. Strangely management stayed hidden until she and the children left the restaurant. They then commended me on my professionalism when dealing with her.

Long story short after three days on this job at the pretzel factory, I walked out. I went to my mom and told her that I couldn't take being talked to and harassed like that anymore. My mom walked out with me. We went into the break room and tried to call the motel room where we lived so Greg could come and pick us up. But the phone kept ringing. My first thought was that he was out in the street as he did before. So my mother and I decided to walk home. It was a hot summer night. I'll say about 15 minutes into walking home it started raining heavy and thundering. As we were walking a thunderbolt came but so close to striking us. I instinctively clung to my mom. I then made a joke about how we would be found burnt to a crisp holding each other. That's me making lemonade out of lemons. In situations like that, it's caused me to believe that maybe my mom did love me. Despite her past actions, I couldn't hold a grudge against her for that long. She did give birth to me for goodness sake.

When we arrived at the motel, surprisingly Greg was there with the children. He acted apologetic that he didn't hear the phone ring. We later discovered that the phone cord had a short. He gave us towels to dry off, hung up our wet clothes, gave us our night clothes and fed us. Working at the book warehouse was okay but we needed a job with a higher pay rate. So my mom and I applied at a mailing house in Moorestown. We were hired with a hourly wage of $1.50 more per hour. Just as things seemed to be going better, we had to move out of the motel. The manager was very kind but explained to us that the owner could be fined if we stayed there any longer. He said that we would have to check out for two weeks and then come back. So we went to the motel up the street. And the environment went from sugar to shit real fast. It turned out that this particular motel was laden with drugs and prostitution. To make matters worse it was infested with mice. We would hang our food from the ceiling by bungee cords in hopes of keeping the mice from eating it. We quickly left that motel and went to another.

This new place was a extended-stay studio. It cost a little more each week but it was well worth it. It was a more sanitary and safer environment. True to his nature Greg started his madness yet again. He had always taken our pay but he started that buying himself gold and expensive cars again. When we got our tax return money that year, he went to Philly and brought his self a four year old Cadillac Coupe. Even at four years old it was still expensive. He wouldn't pick us up from work. On many nights we had to walk home, we didn't even have money to take a taxi. To add insult to injury various girls would call the cell phone that my arduous work paid for and ask to speak to my youngest son. Turned out that he would give girls my son's name instead of his own. His reason for that I'm not sure. He could have made up any name for all that's worth.

Yet again we had to move. It was too many people for the studio room according to management. And that was the largest unit available at that time. So back to Cinnaminson we moved. One day at the gas station we saw Vivian once again. My mother told her of our situation. She let us move into her basement which was a huge blessing for us. Finally a little stability I thought. Now I could enroll my children into school. Which was a big issue with me. I never wanted my children to suffer exploitation the way I did. A part of me believed that if I had been allowed to attend school as I desired, he couldn't have controlled me the way he did. Not that higher education would have instantly freed me. But that there is a great chance that I wouldn't have felt so much self doubt. I could have envisioned my having economic freeness which would have led me to physical and mental freeness a lot sooner. But the fact remained, I didn't have their immunization records, their old school records or even their birth certificates. All of these documents had been lost in storage when he failed to pay the monthly storage fee. Also I didn't have the money to request new documents. I was literally his captive. I couldn't make any moves without his approval and help. So being that it was legal to homeschool, that's what I continued to do. Any adult books on history and culture is what I taught my children from. I made them read the dictionary and some of his old vocabulary building self-help books. As far as math went, I would take blank paper and write down several math problems. Ranging from addition, subtraction, multiplication and division. With science I didn't have any textbooks but they were required to watch the science Channel for at least an hour a day.

It was eerie how my mother and her boyfriend could trick people. Ms. Vivian was a sweet ,godly lady of sound mind. But she truly believed that they were good people. I knew the devils they were. And it sickened me how they could seem to con anyone.

We worked at the mailing house for almost a year around that time. It's funny because my mom and I were the only Americans of African descent working there. There were people from Vietnam, Cambodia, Indonesia and a few Americans of Puerto Rican descent. For me working around immigrants was a learning experience. I wasn't put off the least bit by being around so many foreigners. I've heard so many people say negatives about Asian people but personally I've only had positive experiences with people of Asian ancestry. Initially they were somewhat stand-offish towards me. But after a short time we developed a rapport despite the communication barrier. Once I gained their respect, I found that anyone of my coworkers would have given me the shirt off of their back. I don't know how many countless times my Asian friends offered me half of their food if they thought I was hungry. How many times they gave my mother and I rides home. When we offered them gas money they refused. It reminds me of when we were down south and there was this corner store owned by a South Korean woman. Her name was Sun. She gave us credit for food numerous times. Sadly she was murdered in a robbery gone bad. She left behind a African-American/Korean daughter who was about 10 years old at the time. The police did catch the scum who robbed and killed her a short time later. May Sun rest in peace.

Then there was another Korean woman who taught me how to tell a pregnant woman what sex her child was using only a sewing needle and thread.

Don't ask me how it's done because I can't tell you ,it's a old Asian secret. I may be murdered if I taught you how. Just kidding! But all jokes aside I've learned to take all experiences good and bad, and entwine them into my life lessons.

Another lesson I've learned is how some people smile at you and act very friendly. But they talk about you directly in your face when they think you don't understand their language. I've had 2 Puerto Rican girls on 2 different jobs say that I "look like a monkey". This one girl at the mailing house had just smiled in my face and then seconds later as I'm standing at my table sorting mail. She told her friends, who were also Puerto Rican, that I looked like a monkey. She said it is Spanish of course. This girl attempted to get the other Puerto Rican people in on the joke. But they looked at her like she was crazy. They were too wise to assume that I didn't know any Spanish because I'm black.

It's funny because I've always liked the Spanish language. I've always had a affinity for the Latin culture. I first took Spanish as a elective in the fifth grade. My first childhood crush was a fluent Spanish speaker. His name was José, he was adopted by a well to do Hispanic family. Originally from Guatemala, all the other girls in the class didn't like him. But I thought he was so cute. We would write each other love notes in Spanish class. He spoke very little English so we would have to write each other in Spanish.The usual childish stuff. Do you like me-yes or no.Will you marry me-yes or no.Te gusto- si o no. Quieres casarte conmigo- si o no. At that time I didn't understand the second question but I checked si anyway. I have thought of Jose' several times since adulthood. I've wondered what he's up to now,how he looks as a man,would he recognize me and I he?

When I did talk to this particular girl directly, I let her know that I knew she called me a monkey. I did this in a roundabout manner. I didn't curse her out but I did shame her for her actions. Lesson I learned, that ignorance is universal, audacious and futile. Meanwhile things at home were becoming increasingly intense. The accusations, the interrogations. But it wasn't long before I became pregnant with my youngest child. He immediately started saying that my baby wasn't his child. He accused me of sleeping with any and every Asian coworker. This wasn't true. I believe it was part of his reverse psychology. He thought I wouldn't see all the evils he continued to do because I was so busy defending myself against untrue accusations.

I continued to work at the mailing house throughout my pregnancy. Whenever I had prenatal appointments my mother would accompany me. Even after so many years he still didn't want to acknowledge that he was the father of my children. Most times I will admit that he made sure I took my prenatal vitamins, drank milk, water and pure juice. He also had my bath ready when I got home from work, sometimes. Occasionally he would have my favorite Chinese food waiting for me. I craved Chinese food often with my youngest child. Around this time he started gambling heavy again. Sometimes he won good. But when he lost it was bad. We would have to borrow money from Vivian. I went on temporary disability about two weeks before giving birth.

Despite the stress of my environment, I gave birth to my youngest child October 19. She was born one day after her great maternal grandmother's birthday. Delivered through C-section, she weighed a whopping 9 lbs. 1 oz., my largest baby to date. After born they placed her in neonatal ICU. The doctors explained to me that her white blood cell count was a little high and they wanted to observe her closely. This made me very sad. I began to cry as the doctor said he couldn't guarantee that she could come home with me. Her father went into the neonatal ICU, held her, kissed her and looked deep into her little eyes and prayed for her. When we returned to my room from visiting the baby he said "She'll be in here with you tomorrow by 12 o'clock". I asked what made him think that and he replied "I just know, but you gotta have faith". "Okay" I said. My mom was present during all of this. Again it was difficult for me trying to act normal. You know the grandma, granddad and single young mother scenario. When I knew in my heart my situation was anything but normal.

To my astonishment my daughter was medically cleared that following day as Greg had said. And it was before 12:00 PM when she was brought into my room. We both were released from the hospital three days later. Two weeks later I went back to work. I was receiving temporary benefits from the state and it was a great help (a benefit that I really needed when I lived in Virginia). But Greg decided that wasn't enough. I would make 2 to 3 times that each week. So back to work I went. Reflecting, I realize that he didn't give a damn about me. Despite me holding his secret, despite me having his children, despite me showing him compassion. Even after all the hell he inflicted on me. At that time though I didn't analyze the situation in it's entirety. For some crazy reason I formed the opinion that I needed him, he needed me and our children needed us.

It reminds me of a time when I was 19. He was driving me to work. Now there were a few jeopardies going on here. One, his license was suspended. Two, he didn't have auto insurance. Three, perhaps the most dire. The minivan he had at that time had bad brakes. I worked on the south side of Richmond. Now there are many ways to get there but he chose the way that included many serpentine roads. It was a rich area called Riverside. He thought his chances of getting stopped would be lessened. This area had big beautiful houses that sat on various hills. At the foot or shall I say Valley of those hills, lies the notorious James River. So as he was driving me to work this chilly spring morning, he had his window rolled down.

Now generally I would get fussed at for being cold. This always upset him. And being anemic, I got cold often. But this day he rolled his window up with no complaints. Not even five minutes later, he flipped the van. I mean it rolled over completely. I thought for sure I was dead, as everything went black. Once I came to I then thought he may have died. So I called him and he responded. He asked if I was okay, I then asked if he was okay. Greg then said "Hurry up and get out the car". We didn't have on seatbelts and the van was still flipped on it's roof. He got out and I got out. He started running up the hill saying

"We gotta go". We got to a little park in the area. There we take a break and I asked him "What are you doing"? "Why did you leave"? He told me that he ran because he didn't have a valid drivers license and no auto insurance. I then told him that he shouldn't run because he was only going to make things worse. He then told me that he ran because he would go to jail if the police caught him. Next he asked me to do him a favor. He told me to say that I was driving. He said that because of my age and the fact that I had no criminal or driving record. I would only receive tickets and a small fine but no jail time. I agreed to do as he asked. So we walked back to the van and the police were there on the scene. The police asked were we the owners of the van. We replied yes and then the officer asked what happened. I explained to him that I was driving and I lost control of the van while turning on the curvy road. He asked for my license information and I let him know that I didn't have a license. The officer told me that he was going to have to give me a couple citations. I couldn't be angry with the police officer. He was very pleasant and just doing his job. The officer asked several times did we need a ambulance. We declined each time. The officer went on to say that we were very lucky. He said that people died on that road often. Especially when a vehicle flips. The police officer said that he saw where my head brushed against the driver's side window, (there was a hair oil smear their, I had no oil in my hair that day but Greg did). The officer stated that most people die instantly by breaking their necks when they don't wear seatbelts and have their windows rolled down. Greg then told the officer that he was glad he listened to me because he had his window rolled down right before the accident. The officer then said "You better be glad you listened to her". Shortly thereafter the tow truck arrived and gave us a ride home. I'm so thankful to God because had the van rolled down the hill towards the river. I'm almost certain neither of us would have survived. As usual he promised to pay my fines when I plead guilty and teach me how to drive, which he didn't.

He watched the children each night as I worked at the mailing house. I filled up bottles of breastmilk to last my little girl throughout my work shift. I stayed on this job until my baby was about nine months old. I was laid off right after I asked for and received a raise. After almost 2 years of being a reliable and efficient employee. It was decided that the company couldn't bare to pay me almost $11 an hour. What a pity! So anyway my mom and I were laid off at the same time. In a short time we found another job. This time at a warehouse that shipped out art, hobby and craft supplies to various stores nationwide. We had to undergo a drug screen, aptitude test and physical. We passed all three. I started this job by myself three days before my mother. It was really intense. On my breaks I had to call and stay on the phone with Greg. The most I was allowed to do was buy a bag of chips and soda out of the vending machine. If I were a minute late calling that would be a major issue when I got home. So I knew better than to disobey his orders. My mom joined me a few days later, which pleased him. Because now he had her to watch me and report to him anything someone may have said to me. I really enjoyed working on this job. It was fast-paced and challenging. After fully trained I was allowed to work independently. I had plans of that becoming my career job as it paid well and provided opportunities for advancement. A downside though was when I got home each evening, I was questioned to the third degree. There were black, white, Puerto Rican and Asian guys there who liked me. But I've never let that get to my head. I'd be damned if I would catch a beat down behind flirting back with these guys. I am guilty of being naive, aloof and maybe slow to react but I've never been stupid.

I recall this one time when some Hispanic guy had just been hired there. For the first week or so, each time he saw me he would speak. I would ignore him each time and each time when I got home (me being the honest person) would tell him. So one day he came to the job to bring me some food on my break. On my way back into the warehouse, this same Hispanic guy was standing outside smoking a cigarette. As I was about to enter the building, I threw my trash into the trashcan outside the door, as I normally would. When I got home that evening there was a big argument. He accused me of sleeping with this guy. In his delusional mind I acted unnatural. He drilled me with "Why didn't you walk far away from him"? I reminded him that the guy was standing by the door and that was the only entrance. Had I walked further away, he would have said that I had something to hide. He would've said that I didn't want him to see the guy talking to me. This argument consisted of yelling, name-calling and shoving. He didn't throw any blows because I had to be back to work early the next a.m. I tell you I couldn't win for losing. This was a vicious cycle that I could never get out of. This kind of ill treatment went on each day after work. It became a part of life for me. I missed being around my children often but the only peace I got was when I worked. Shortly things went from bad to worse.

Just when I found a job I really loved. A job I envisioned myself being for a long time. I was in a car accident that left me with permanent injuries, out of work and forced to be around him 24-7. A short time after the accident we moved back into a hotel. It turned out that Vivian's daughter and grandsons needed to move back in with her. My mother and Greg remained friends with Ms. Vivian. Though it sickened me how Ms. Vivian thought the sun rose and set on Greg. She had not a clue of the monster he was. The car we had at the time was totaled because of the accident. My mother had full coverage. I thank God I wasn't killed.

Because of the permanent injuries, I had the grounds to sue. I went through years of physical therapy, injections and surgery, all to no avail. Some procedures I had only exacerbated my injuries. My mother was driving and she herself suffered injuries as well. Each time I had to go to a doctor's appointment, Greg was almost always present. There were a few times when he sent my mom to watch me.

After years of bumbling from hotel to hotel, motel to motel. They finally got an apartment. Initially I was happy. Finally a chance for my children to have a stronger sense of stability after moving to New Jersey. We first were informed of the apartment by a church that my mom sought some assistance from. The apartment was privately owned by a member of the church. So they gave this person (an elderly black man) our contact information. Several days later he contacted my mom and asked her about her financial situation and such. It so happened that Thanksgiving was a couple of days away. So he offered to pay for us to go out and eat Thanksgiving dinner. My mother accepted and he and his wife arrived on Thanksgiving afternoon to drive us there. He paid for my mom, my three youngest children and me. He went inside, paid and then dropped us off. He gave my mother his cell phone number so she could call him to pick us up. My mom's boyfriend chose to stay in the background. A couple of days after that the owner picked up my mother and I along with a couple of the children. He drove us to the property so we could look at it. When we entered the apartment it was in shambles. There were clothes and trash everywhere. Old broken furniture and no electricity. We had to use a couple of flashlights that he provided to look around. We drew the blinds but that was of no use. The position of the apartment didn't allow for much sunlight to enter. Despite the appearance of the apartment, how could we object? We needed a more stable environment like yesterday.

When we arrived back at the hotel, we had to go through a series of questions. Most involving sexual content. "Did he touch y'all"? "Did he rape y'all"? "Did he ask for sex"? "Did you give him sex to get the apartment"? No, no, no, no and no! No a 1000 times, but that never sufficed with him. About a couple weeks later we had saved the first months rent and deposit. This is when we moved in.

At first it seemed like things could maybe get brighter. We all were happy to have an apartment. Me being optimistic only caused me to be delusional, especially in this situation. In the midst of me going to doctors, therapy and dealing with my injuries. I had to deal with his excessive rage. No matter what

I did it was never enough. He would take the smallest of situations and blow them out of proportion. Not only that, he would bring up things that may have happened years ago and act as if it just happened.

And truth is, it was nothing to be upset about to begin with. If I had a nickel for every time he re-questioned me about all the various jobs I've had since the age of 16. I would have a nice nest of money and I don't mean that figuratively. The oldest of my brothers had left home when he was 16. So that left my baby brother, baby sister, my children, my mother, her boyfriend and myself. I continued homeschooling my children. I would press periodically about when he was going to let me get the necessary documents to enroll them in school. As always he had some way of brushing me off. Sometimes he would say "Oh, when I get some extra money or when you get paid". Other times he would belittle me and make me to feel stupid saying things like "What is education"? "Some of the greatest people didn't have a formal education, Jesus didn't have a education". "You a stupid ass bitch that don't know how to use your mind"! "Everything they need to know can be taught right here in this apartment. I don't want my children to be brainwashed". Enough said, that kind of diatribe would shut me up for a while. And it inflicted an horrific blow to my self-esteem especially when said in front of the whole family.

When I wasn't going to appointments, I was made to stay in the house. I could leave out if he went with me. Or on very rare occasions, I could go without him but I always had to have an escort. If a man spoke to me I couldn't speak back or I would be accused of wanting to bed him. With this kind of treatment I didn't want to go out. I figured at least he can't accuse me and start arguments if I'm in the confines of the apartment. Wrong! He started accusing me of sleeping with my brother! Can you believe? This sicko actually acted as if he believed that.

Once I became disabled my core job (as far as domestic duties) was the primary cook for the whole family. I would cook and serve everyone in the family. Well, after a while he forbade me from plating my little brothers food. Either my mother or my sister had to. I did that and I thought okay may be no more false allegations. Wrong! He then said that I couldn't cook for him period. I thought okay, well he can't pick arguments with me now. Wrong! My sister took the reins of cooking solely for our brother. No problem but guess what? He started accusing her.

I recall one time when he and my youngest brother were sitting down playing video games. I was sitting on the sofa beside Greg. I would have rather been somewhere else in the apartment but he ordered me to sit beside him and watch him play video games. I got use to these absurd orders because if there was one thing that I didn't want to do, it was cause any ripples with him. I for the most part became a zombie to his every whim. Looking back I realize that it was my way of surviving.

So he and my brother were joking about kicking each others butt referring to the video game. I chuckled at the comments and said to my brother "You're in trouble now". Within minutes he calmly turned off the game, sent my brother into his room, close the windows and blinds. He called my middle son into the front room to get him a extension cord. Meanwhile I'm sitting there trying to figure out what was going on. He coldly said to me "You think I'm stupid, I saw that shit you did. I saw you wink at him". I explained to him that I didn't wink and that he was mistaken. After my son got him the extension cord. He tackled and hog tied me. I was crying and begging him to stop. Letting him know that I would never do anything like that. When he had me subdued, he got the fillet knife from the kitchen and started poking me in my midsection with just the very tip. Not deep enough to penetrate. But enough to hurt and cause terror, not knowing if the next poke would penetrate deeply. Meanwhile my children, siblings and mother were in the back room. This went on for some time, I'm not sure exactly how long. After he finished with this torture session, he cut the extension cord off of me. He told me to never do him wrong and acted as if nothing happened. I was in complete dismay and traumatized. This was the first time he had tied me up and tortured me but it wasn't the last.

There was this other time when he started to accuse me of cheating (something he always did when he wanted to justify his abuse) and forced me to drink a large amount of this fruit flavored liquor that was 80 proof. He had a knife to my side while my hands were tied behind my back. As we sat on the mattress that was on the floor. He told me to hold my head back and open my mouth, which I did. He then poured the liquor into my mouth and told me to swallow, which I did. He then started asking me a series of questions all relating to fidelity. He poured more alcohol into my mouth. After several pours like this I broke down and started crying hysterically. I could barely sit up, my eyes rolled to the back of my head, I felt as if I was about to fade. Honestly I thought I was going to die. All I could say was "oh God". Apparently he thought I was going to die as well because he went and filled up a bucket of cold water and threw it on me. He then got my mom to fill up several glasses of water. He held one of the glasses to my mouth and told me to swallow. He then untied my hands and next stuck his fingers in my throat which caused me to throw up. He gave me more water and repeated this until he felt that all the alcohol was out of my stomach. I believe that was his way of trying to give me truth serum. My mother was always close by but she never did much to stop him.

After about two years of treatment, I was discharged from my doctors. Not long after, I received a settlement of $35,000. After the lawyer fees and bills I walked with $17,000. That whole situation was yet another level of hell. He would have me call the attorney 2 sometimes 3 times a day. Asking questions about how much money I could expect, how long would it take to receive payment etc. I felt so bad because he had me asking the dumbest repetitive questions. The lawyers must have thought I was retarded. To make matters worse, he would be right there as I was on the phone. Listening to my every word. I had to ask exactly what and how he wanted me to. There were many times when I had to write down what he wanted me to ask. During the whole process he had me fire at least two attorneys because he didn't like the responses they gave. They didn't say what he wanted to hear. I caught quite a few black eyes because he thought I talked too nice to the lawyers.

So after all is said and done. I finally got the check and cashed it. My mom's boyfriend was there every step of the way. I thought that this money would be my way out. I pled with him to allow me to get a bank account but he wouldn't. He had control of all my money. Without that I couldn't get my freedom. He slept with the money on his side of the bed underneath the mattress. So many nights I thought of how I could get the children, get the money and sneak out. But I could think of no way to get out with everyone and not wake him up. I would think to myself "Where am I going to go"? "Where am I going to live"? I didn't know how to drive, I didn't have any family in New Jersey.Once more fear struck me and won. Fear gripped me like a bat to darkness.

Greg was never happy. After a few months he decided that he wanted to go to Atlantic City to try and flip the money. I was against it but what could I do. I was powerless to do anything to stop him. He made me go with him. Before going there he vowed to be careful and walk away if he wasn't winning. When we got there he made me sit at a slot machine. He didn't want me to be at the table with him. But I had to stay within view of him and let him know when I had to use the restroom. Then he would look at the time and give me a time limit to be back. Usually it was a 10 minute limit. Once back I had to let him know and then return to the appointed slot machine. After a while gambling, he came and gave me $500 of my own money. I wanted to purchase a hooked on phonics system for my children. So that they could advance their reading skills.

A short time after that he came and told me to go outside with him. I asked was he okay. He didn't answer but said "How much money you got"? "Give me the money". I thought that he was joking initially. I said "Well you have plenty of money". He responded with "No I don't, they got me"! I began to cry and asked "How could you do that to children? I trusted you". He said "I don't care about all that, give me the money". I said "No" and I hit him on his arm. He coldly laughed in my face. So I'll admit, I attempted to hit him in his face. To hit him where it hurt. As I threw my fist he turned his head to avoid it. Somehow my thumbnail lightly scratched his cheek. He became enraged and started hitting me in my stomach, head and arms. He pulled a couple of my kinky twist out (a hairstyle they uses extensions braided into natural hair). All of this transpired on the side of the Hilton Casino. I guess all the security and cameras didn't spot this. He then took my pocketbook and ripped it apart. All of my contents were thrown everywhere in an attempt to find the money. Little did he know I had tucked it away in my bra. He told me to stop crying before I got him into trouble. So I stopped crying. We walked to the valet area of the casino. He told me that if I didn't give him the money, that I shouldn't go back home .Because he was going to fuck me up when I got back home. I then reached into my bra and gave him $300 in 20's. He asked me how much money it was. I told him $300. He then purposely let go of the money and said "Bitch, I want it all, not no damn 300 of it". It was a very windy night and 20s were flying everywhere. I couldn't retrieve one bill. People in the valet area must have thought it was their lucky day. All I could do was just stand there and watch. I couldn't get upset with the employees or patrons. Who wouldn't pick up loose money that just blew their way? I eventually gave him the rest, with the exception of about $30. I didn't want to get stuck out there. After several more hours there of back-and-forth gambling, he decided that it was time for us to go home. Thank God we had plenty of food and our bills paid up to date. I was due another payment of $800. I received this as part of my lost wage claim on a biweekly basis. I received that check about three days later.

My mother cashed it as he didn't want me to leave the house. When my mom got back, she gave it directly to him. Not that it would have made any difference if she gave it to me, I had no power to stop him. He decided that he would take my money and go to Atlantic city. But this time he was taking my mom. He had a habit of blaming me when he lost the money. He said that I had a negative energy because I would just sit at the slots and read a magazine. However when my mother went, she would order all kinds of drinks and get sloshed. It seems that she never cared about financial stability or stability of any kind. No, she never cared about stupid stuff like that. Give her alcohol, a Percocet and sex and she'd sell out her own daughters in a flash.

He and my mother left to go to A.C later that day. That was the most peace I had in a long time. They stayed gone for about a day. When they returned home they both reeked of alcohol and looked beat. I asked how he did and he replied "Not good, I might have to take your perfume back".

You see when I first received the settlement, he let me get something that I wanted. I had a few clothes but didn't need many because I rarely left out. I wore my hair in braids, so I couldn't think of anything but perfume. So that's what it was. A $70 bottle of Dior J'adore. I had the receipt in my wallet. I pled with him not to take it back. I explained to him that we had food and our bills were paid. And that he got his check the following week.

They had gotten back in the early hours of the morning, before the sun rose. After talking to him for several minutes I went to go back to sleep, he went to go to sleep as well. Some hours later I was awakened by the phone ringing. I went and answered it. My sister was on the other end. I asked her where she was and what was she doing. She informed me that her, my oldest daughter and mother had taken the bus to the mall to return my perfume. We ended our conversation and hung up. I then shook Greg awake and asked him "How could you be such a rat"? "You went into my pocketbook while I was sleep, took the receipt and my perfume back". "After all of my money you lost, after all the pain I'm in each day. All I had to show for it was a bottle of perfume and you took that back"! Sometimes I lost my mind like that. By questioning his lack of integrity. Being that he was sleepy, he didn't give a response to my statement. He just said "Leave me the fuck alone" I said "No, you owe me an explanation" and kept asking him why. He then got out of the bed and went into the room with the children and shut the door. I followed and knocked on the door. I tried to open the door but it was locked. Realizing that the children were still asleep, I stopped knocking and stepped into the next bedroom. Minutes passed as I'm standing in the threshold of the next bedroom. He opened the door of the bed room he was in with the children. I went towards that bedroom and before I could get my other foot past that bedroom's threshold, I felt a large object hit my head. I blacked out for a short time. I recovered to find my children's wooden rocking horse beside me. I got up stunned and woozy. Crazy thing is I didn't feel any pain but I felt something running down my face. I went to the bathroom and looked into the mirror. I had the deepest, widest laceration on my left eyebrow. The sight of it made me want to faint. He came running to the bathroom apologizing saying that he thought I was trying to hurt him. I started crying saying that he " damaged my face, I got to get stitches". He said "You'll be okay, please don't tell on me"! He then went and got some beeswax to put on my cut. A little while later, my mother and the girls return home.

He told his version of what happened but my mother wasn't concerned one way or the other. So he concocts this story about what to tell the doctors what had happened. He told me to tell them that I was going into the cabinet and a ceramic plate slipped out of my hands while trying to remove it and cut my eyebrow. So I stuck with that fabricated scenario of events. When I got to the ER, the triage nurse asked me if I was being abused. I lied and said no because I just didn't trust anyone. At that time I had formed a cynical outlook on society. In my mind I thought no one really cared.

It turned out that I needed 75 stitches, 75 stitches. The girls were sent with me to make sure I stuck to the script. When I got home he had this look of contentment on his face. He seemed pleased with his self. That I now had a permanent scar on my face. His reaction shouldn't have surprised me. That was the lamest excuse saying that he thought I was going to hurt him. If that were the case then why didn't he keep the door locked? Why would he unlock and open the door to entice me to enter? I had never caused any harm to him before even though he deserved it. After he wounded me so badly, he helped me in the healing process. He brought scar pads to put on it. He cared for it and even took the stitches out because he didn't want me to go back to the ER. But each time he tended to it he had this smirk on his face. So one day I asked "Why are you smiling"? He responded with "I'm so happy that it's not going to keloid from the looks of it".

To this day I'm convinced that I walked into a trap. And if that wasn't bad enough he went back to the casino a week later and lost all his money. When he and my mother returned home, he was very angry with me for no reason as always. He sent me into the children's room. Minutes later he came into the room and sent the children out. He went to their closet and got a tennis racket out. He started yelling at me. Asking me why did I scratch him on his face. He started saying that I was jealous of him and that I tried to destroy his face when he and I were in Atlantic City. Not only was this scratch very light but it had completely disappeared. It had happened at that point about two weeks before. I wouldn't be surprised if my mother was behind the attack. She seemed to get off at the sight of violence. And she has been known to incite him particularly when it came to me.

I begged him not to hit me. I cried and prayed to no avail. He still started beating me on my legs with the wood part that surrounded the net of the racket. He held it like a baseball bat. My mom was standing there the whole time watching and was mostly quiet. It was the most painful beating. This pain was severe. I was screaming and calling to God. He mimicked me and said "Uh huh, you ain't call God when you scratched my face". After some minutes which seemed like forever, my mom said "Okay Greg, she had enough". He hit me several more times and then threw the racket across the room. I was so traumatized. The next day I couldn't walk and my legs had turned from red to literally black in color, no exaggeration. He made me wear long pants around the house to try and conceal what he did to me. My children didn't speak to me about it but they weren't stupid.

That kind of behavior was typical of him. I recall another time when my mom and the girls had left to take care business. As soon as they left he tackled me and started smacking me. Saying that I was going to tell him who I slept with on the many jobs I had. He then went to the kitchen and got a chef knife. He pinned me down on the sofa, took the knife and started thrusting it as if he was going to stab me all over my face. The knife came within centimeters of my face. He cut out a couple of my braids with the knife. As if that wasn't enough, he went and heated up a fork over the gas stove. He then burned me on my rear end with the fork. He then decided that he'd rather burn me with the knife. So he heated the chef knife and burned my legs with it. I had multiple blisters on my legs and fork marks on my behind. The fork marks I still have on my rear as well as some dark spots on my legs from the knife burns.

For a week or so after that, whenever I closed my eyes and attempted to drift off to sleep, I had flashbacks of him over me with the knife. As with the tennis racket attack and so many other brutal wounds he inflicted on me, they healed on the outside but mentally I haven't. I still suffer for flashbacks on occasion.

No matter how much precaution I took I could never win. I recall one time when he was telling me that I had to call it find a lawyer for my mom.

She was also in the accident but the insurance company has stopped her PIP benefits. According to him my mom couldn't handle business affairs properly. I was dumb but a little smarter than her. The only true intelligent one in the household was him and he didn't let anyone forget it. He went through great lengths to crush our self-esteem.

So anyway he'll started ranting and raving about how I better find my mom a lawyer in the next five minutes or he was going to fuck me up. So I got out the Yellow Pages and started looking for lawyer that specialized in the insurance field. It was around 4:30 in the afternoon. So I was moving as fast as possible. While I was trying to call he was in the background fussing about how stupid I was etc. I then asked if I could go into another room and call. He said "No, you gonna keep your fat ass right here and call. You're going to stay in here where I can listen to you". So I said "Okay but could you be quiet while I'm making the call"? He went off and said "You uncle Tom bitch, I'm in my house. I ain't gonna be quite". "I ain't gonna be quiet in my own house for no white man. Only your good for nothing uncle Tom ass would expect me to do that". I just stayed quiet as time was passing. I just wanted to speak with someone so he wouldn't "fuck me up". I called this one number and the phone rang. He noticed that I was on the phone and said "Bitch, you gonna be calling lawyers why I'm in the background fussing? What the fuck is wrong with you"? He ran over and pressed the button to hang up the phone, went into the closet, got a metal pole and hit me on my left arm close to my wrist. It hurt so bad and I still have a permanent lump there to this day. I speculate that it may have been fractured though I never got it x-rayed.

It seemed that one of his main goals was not only to be evil but to destroy who I am as a person, my core. He would for no reason send me out of the room with him and into the room with the children. In an attempt to reduce me to a child or I guess he assumed that it was punishment. But truth be told any time I was allowed away from him the better I felt. I recall once when he banished me out of the room. I was all too happy to comply. I took my books, portable CD player, CD's and pocketbook. Not five minutes later he came into the room and with his bare hands, broke all my CD's and CD player. As well as my pocketbook. He ripped my only pocketbook. I said absolutely nothing to warrant his anger. Like a good little girl, I had calmly walked into the other room. He was always on a quest to steal my joy. Always trying to kill me, spiritually. After he destroyed my property, I sat on the bed and cried. Asking God why? Why is he so evil to me? I then lie down on the bed crying and asked God the same question- why? At that moment a voice came to me and said that he wants to break your spirit. That was the answer! Seconds later the ceiling fan spun one full rotation, my children also witnessed this. Mind you there was no power going to it and no wind stirring anywhere in the room. As a matter of fact that fan hadn't been turned on for months. Some of you reading this may think that I'm crazy or at least was delusional at that point. But the message was very clear and very real. Was it God or my higher self? You be the judge on what you believe, but I will stick to what I know.

It's funny how I would be made aware of things. Like once I had this dream that my brother (the oldest of the two) was locked up. In my dream he had on a orange jumpsuit. This was a lucid dream. My mother wanted to know where he was. He had left home at 16 years old. She called him and he called her ever so often. But she hadn't spoken to him for a couple weeks. So the next day after the dream, I told Greg about it. He immediately said "Jan (my mom's nickname) call the jail, that's where Greg III is". And sure enough that's where he was. Turned out that he had got into a fight with some guy and was charged with assault. I even dreamt that Greg's grandmother visited me and apologized for all the wrong she did. I later found out that she had died about a month before I had this dream. I relayed this message to Greg and told him that she was sorry for her actions. He didn't want to hear it. He said that no matter what I said he still hated her, even in her death. Things like this I couldn't make happen, they just did. And it wasn't that often.

After being in this apartment for some time, we were evicted. With his gambling habit, habit of not paying bills and basically dealing with a slumlord. Anyone could guess that we wouldn't live there that long. We moved into another apartment just across the walkway. So we moved into the new apartment and it wasn't much better than the dump we previously lived in. But it was a roof over our head. My mom's boyfriend made the usual promises. He said that he was going to pay the bills, be a good father and role model for the boys, he was going to stop gambling yada yada yada.

After me still being unable to work, Greg decided that I should apply for social security and I agreed. I must admit I was discouraged because of my young age. In the meanwhile things went along as usual. The arguments, the physical and verbal abuse, the gambling. He had a heart attack sometime in 2001 or early 2002. When he had it I didn't believe it. I was at home with the children when my mom called me and told me what happened. Long story short he collapsed in the hospital, almost died and had to be transported to a hospital they could handle his situation. He received a couple of stents and lived to be evil another day. I truly believed that his near-death experience would transform him for the better. It was unclear at that time what caused the heart attack. The doctors have speculations but nothing concise. So years later, while he gambled, I sat down reading a newspaper as I normally did. I noticed this ad in a New York newspaper. It was posted by a large law firm located in North Jersey. This ad asked did you or someone you love suffer a heart attack while taking Vioxx? Eureka that's it, that's what caused his heart attack years earlier. He was taking Vioxx at that time. He had been prescribed this medication by his orthopedic doctor. He had a very bad case of degenerative osteoarthritis in his knee and Vioxx was the only thing that took away his pain. I was happy to report this information to him. He often accused me of poisoning him, which I didn't of course. I wanted to believe that if I treated him kindly and showed undying loyalty (even though not deserved) he had no option but to treat me kindly back. Boy was I gullible! As a matter of fact the nicer I treated him the more he hated me. He didn't trust me that much more because deep inside his tiny heart, he knew that all he really deserved from me was pure hate- simple and plain. Anyway he left it to me to make all the phone calls as well as filling out paperwork. I completed an information packet from the lawyers about 30 pages thick on his behalf. He swore to me that when he did receive compensation ,he would pay me back most of my settlement money that he had lost as well as help me get my license,a car and an apartment. So believing him yet again I worked hard to assist him in every way. I became his at home paralegal. Every document sent to him he had me read over and fill out for him.

Meanwhile I was denied for Social Security. After that time I hired a lawyer. He filed for me to have a hearing in front of a judge. It took a little over a year before the actual hearing was held. I know some of you reading this are pondering, why did she tolerate this? Why didn't she just go to the police? But what you must understand is that, this life was all I knew. I was use to this treatment. I had no trust in anyone outside of my worst enemies, my mom and her boyfriend. I had no trust in any system, any shelter or any organization. And a part of me was concerned with what my children would think of me. What would they think of mommy if she were the cause of daddy being sent away from them for a very long time? They knew of the physical abuse towards me by their father, I'm sure. Though I went through great lengths to cover black eyes and bruises many times. The sexual abuse they were unaware of. I didn't want my children to feel any guilt as to how they came to be. They never questioned how did mommy have her first child at 14 and daddy is 15 years older than her? They never questioned how is it that our daddy is also our aunt and uncles' daddy? This whole scenario is all too twisted. I certainly didn't want them to know the pain of not having their father around as I did. I blamed my father for all the abuse I suffered. If he hadn't abandoned me, then these things would never have happened. I was also petrified that if I were ever to date,then this would be companion would attempt to molest and rape my children as I had been. So as long as his anger and abuse were directed towards me, as long as he acted like he loved the children, I carried the burden of agony. Deep in my heart I knew I would escape, somehow, someway. No matter how depressed I was, there was always a glimmer of hope.

After years of negotiations, Merck settled. Each claimant got different amounts of compensation. If a person smoked,were overweight or had high blood pressure they were deemed already high risk for a heart attack according to Merck's lawyers. Nonetheless valid documented claims were paid. My mother's boyfriend received his settlement. When he got it the first thing he brought was a $12,000 Rolex for himself. I suggested that he get a car and us a better apartment to live in or even purchase a townhouse. He liked to cut me in half with his verbal lashing. "Bitch, I almost died from a heart attack you didn't. This is what I want and what I deserve. I'm buying this Rolex, fuck you". I mean call me silly, but I just thought it unwise to be living in the ghetto. Walking around in the ghetto with a watch that cost the price of some cars. Standing at the bus stop with a real Rolex on. While your many children are sharing two-bedrooms and he and I were using the front room as a third. You know he didn't do any of what he promised. He told me to go fuck myself when I mentioned what he promised. He let it be known that his name was on the check not mine. According to him that was his money to do whatever he wanted and he wasn't going to give me shit. I was lost for words, speechless. Like my soul had left my body for second or so. I was so hurt, after all I was the person who told him about it and filled out his paperwork. It was like my body turned off all emotion or reaction to keep from snapping. I just opened my mouth, shook my head and couldn't utter a word. After the initial shock wore off, a voice came to me and said "that's all right one day you'll have the money needed to get away and your name will be on the check".

He became increasingly paranoid. He put the sofa in front of the door each night. He put bungee cords on the front storm door and hooked the other end to a nail that he hammered into the front room window sill. He also nailed the bedroom windows shut. When ever we wanted something to eat or drink we had to get his permission first. I was made to urinate in a bucket that he placed in the front room corner. If I got up to go to the bathroom he would accuse me of sneaking out. Even still I had to wake him up each time I used the bucket. Or I would have hell to pay the next day. And I knew better than to lie and say I didn't get up when I did. That would only make his wrath worse. Yes every day was a waking hell! And I was accustomed to it.

Whatever I wanted to watch on television he would dissect, analyze and shame me from watching it. And trust me I wanted to watch alot of television. It was my only way of escaping. He shamed me from reading. Whether magazines, newspapers, books etc. he had something negative to say. Sometimes when he got extra money from gambling, he would buy me new clothes, shoes, pocketbooks or perfume. I would accept it and thank him. I would then just keep most of it in the closet as I had nowhere to wear them. He would then say "Why don't you wear your new stuff? Won't you wear your new clothes or use your new pocketbook". With his insistence I did just that. And just as I began to attempt some level of happiness through material means, he took it all back. This cycle he repeated over and over.

Around this time he brought a puppy. It was a cute six week old silky terrier. He let me name him. So I named him Gaupo (handsome in Spanish). For the first few weeks he was okay with the puppy. But after some time he began to hate him. He was so adamant on controlling the dog. When ever the children or I gave him a command he adhered. Whenever Greg gave him a command he rebelled. I tried to explain to Greg that it was the monotone he used. Whenever you talked pleasant to him, he would obey. My mom's boyfriend said that he wasn't going to sweet talk a dog. He said that he's feeding him and he's going to listen to him no matter how he says it. So he went to war with the poor dog. Hitting him with a newspaper, pushing him around, kicking him. He even punched the dog in the face a few times. I spoke up on behalf of the dog, begging him not to mistreat Gaupo. After the first few times of my protest do you know what Greg accused me of? You're not going to believe this! He accused me of beastiality!! Now did he believe this madness or saying this in an attempt to defile my character, reflecting I believe the latter.

After months of Gaupo not submitting, he walked him out of the apartment and let him go. I'm just finding out from my oldest son that he picked him up by his leash, swung him around and threw him across the train tracks. My son is convinced that Gaupo died and so am I. I'm starting to cry as I'm writing this. Greg's virulent ways knew no boundaries.

After over a year of record gathering and all the other stuff that lawyers do in preparation for a hearing. My lawyer wrote to inform me of the pending hearing date,this added to my stress. I never fancied being in front of judges even though this was different. And I wasn't enthused about the chance of being rejected again, though I had substantial records and evidence. Right before the hearing, my mom's boyfriend added to my despair. Telling me that if the judge didn't tell me I was approved right then, that meant I would be denied. He told me that after the hearing I would come home crying because he was angry with me. If I ever crossed or angered him I would pay. I wouldn't be blessed according to him. So at the end of the hearing the judge said that he would render his decision on a later date. I spoke with my lawyer (a very good lawyer may I add, the top in the field) and he said that this was normal and that I shouldn't be alarmed. So when I got home I explained everything to Greg. He said "I told you that you wasn't gonna get approved. That's what happens when you fuck wit me". After him saying this I began to cry. He then said "I told you that you was gonna be crying after the hearing".

After a short time, I believe it was somewhere between 4 to 6 weeks later, I received my award letter. It detailed the grounds for which I was approved, when it became effective and how much retroactive pay I was to receive as well as my monthly benefits. It took another 6-8 weeks to receive the check. Greg didn't allow me to have a bank account. So I cashed it with him right there on my neck.

We didn't have personal transportation so I suggested that we get a minivan or something large enough to accommodate the family. He was totally against a minivan. He found a SUV more desirable. So he and I sought to buy a SUV within the set price range. I knew that we needed transportation in order for me to get myself free and away from him. He finally found a Escalade that was in excellent condition.It had low mileage and a good price. He wanted to finance the vehicle. I thought it would be better to just buy it and have some form of ownership. After I expressed why I thought it would be more intelligent to buy it cash and the benefits of it, he agreed. So he began negotiating with the salesman. He tried to talk the dealer down on the price but the dealer didn't budge but $500. So when they were about to close the deal Greg sent me outside. I didn't want to go because I thought it was another set up for him to accuse me of bedding every man in town. So I said "Why do you want me to go outside, I don't want you to accuse me later on". He said "I won't, I promise"." I want you to keep an eye on the car while they inspect it, I don't want them to try and hide something that may be wrong with it". I said "Okay then". And went to watch the Escalade. When it came time to count out all the money, he came and got me for assistance. After the money was counted he sent me back out. He was in the sales office I know for least two hours. They did all kinds of paperwork. Finally after hours of me sitting in the SUV, he came out and handed me a small stack of paperwork. I looked through it before placing it in the glove compartment. I noticed that the bill of sales had only his name on it. I asked "Why is my name not on the receipt, when my money paid for it". He said that it was just a receipt and that it didn't matter. I pressed a little more and said "Are you telling me that they refused to put my name on the receipt"? He said "Well I told them to put your name on the bill of sales and they said that in New Jersey it's illegal to sell a person a car without a license". I said "Okay, but couldn't I be a co- buyer"? He said "Look that's what they told me, you wanna go back and talk to them about it"? I said "Naw,thats okay". He then said "Don't worry, your name is going to be the title". I asked him later that night when did he plan on helping me get my license. He said "Well, you gotta know how to drive first". I said "Okay, I know that but". He said "I'll take you first thing Saturday morning, I'll take you to an empty school parking lot". I felt a little warmer inside. I thought it won't be long now, I'm one step closer to freedom. There wasn't much money left after buying the vehicle. But I had filed for benefits on behalf of my children. And this money was going to be what I used to leave. Being a mother of five, I knew that I couldn't act too hasty. Because if I didn't act smart, it could affect my children. And my children are and were my utmost concern. So I had to pull my hand easy out of the lions mouth. What the old folks would say.

About six weeks later he received the title in the mail. And guess what? You already know. My name wasn't on the title, only his. Legally I had no grounds, no say so. No say so in something that I solely paid for. I thought about the epiphany I had when he received his settlement. And those words were coming to pass. That's all right I thought. The next check I receive is going to be the money I use to make my break.

When I received the other payments, he was there, just as he always was. When I had the cash he was the nicest to me. He told me that was my money and that he didn't want any of it. He said that I had done so much for him already. I asked him if I could get a bank account. He said "Yeah, you can get a bank account and I'm going to get one with you. We can have one joint account and then you can have your own personal account. I think you're smart to really want to get a bank account. Do you know what bank you're dealing with"? "No", I replied. "Well, after you research what's the best bank for your needs, you let me know and I'll take you there. We'll open our accounts at the same time". "All right", I replied. He did a lot to rock me to sleep. He spoke a lot of nice pleasant adages, professing how he really changed this time. He even let me sleep with the money under my side of the mattress. He let me know "I don't have anything to hide, if I try to take that money while you're asleep you're gonna wake up right". "Yeah", I replied. "All right then, I told you that I'm on the up and up". I wanted so many times to take my children and sneak out with the money. But sneaking out was impossible, he had the fort locked down. And leaving while he was out of the house was out of the question. He strategically took one or two of the children each time he left out. I couldn't abandon not one of my babies. So I had to wait for the right moment. After his short-lived spurt of goodness, he started gambling again. He vowed to gamble with his own money and not ask me for a dime, like I had a choice. Sometimes the best way to control a slave is to make them think that they have options. Being the product of captivity, you can bet that they will always choose the option that suits the captor.

So after I'll say a week or so of back-and-forth in Atlantic City, he came back telling me to give him my money. I said "No, this is the children's money and I want to get somewhere to stay with this". "You already took all of my other money ,this is not fair"." How do you ever expect to be blessed if you keep mistreating me"? "Bitch, give me the money. I'm not playing with you. Give it to me now or you gonna have hell to pay". I still refused and sat on the bed in an attempt to block him. He pushed me over without much effort. Now I have never been a frail woman but his strength and girth surpassed mine a great deal. So when he got the bag of money, I grabbed it and held on to it for dear life. Making myself as heavy as possible. Minutes of pushing, pulling and crying pasted and I then finally gave up. After having conquered, he stood over me and said "Now, you're going with me". "No, I don't want to go with you" I replied. "Look, I said you're going with me". "Okay", I said. But little did he know I had my mind made up. If he lost this money as he had before, I wouldn't have to deal with any more pain. I went into the medicine cabinet and took all of the Xanax I could find. Some were mine prescribed by my doctor, some were my mothers' prescribed by her doctor. I poured them all into one bottle. I know it had to be at least 120 one milligram pills. I put the bottle in my pocket and kept my plan to myself.

So we got to A.C and he wanted me to stay in the Escalade while he and my brother went in to gamble. Normally I would have been distressed about staying in the car by myself but in my mind it didn't matter because I had my plan. And I was almost sure that he was going to lose my money, I had a gut feeling. After sitting in the car for at least an hour, I went to see how he was doing. When I got inside I went to the blackjack tables, he was already down to a couple of thousand dollars. He went from $25,000 to $2000 in that short time. True to his nature he lied and said that he had the rest in his pockets. He told me to go back out to the car, which I did. I'll say about 20 or 30 minutes later, he and my brother came walking to the car. He got in and hastefully pulled off. A little ways up the street he started blaming me for him losing all of the money. I mean cursing, name-calling and yelling. I was just flabbergasted at his guile. He would create whole scenarios to tell one lie or shift the blame on his victims for his evil doings. Just as he did so many years earlier when I told my mother how he was raping me. He said that I was lying in an attempt to break them up (I repeated this). He had a way of look-ing at someone like he was going to kill them. You could feel this energy and would instantly become petrified. My mother wasn't much better than him. Using his twisted, sick, perverted pedophiliac lust for me to her advantage. Telling him that if he left her she would go to the police and tell them that he was "Fucking my daughter". Even the terminology she used was obscene. She knew very well what he was doing all those years ago when I was a child. And what he was doing to me as an adult. She made no efforts to protect me. Sometimes I would vent to her about my anguish. About what he did to me as a child. And she would sit there and tell me that one day I'll be happy. That one day I'll be away from him. That one day God will make him pay for all the evil he inflicted on the whole family. And at that moment, just that moment I believed she was genuine. I felt sorry for her because I saw her as a victim as well. I thought maybe years of torture and abuse had distorted her way of thinking. Or maybe she was just as fearful as I was of being a single mother. I had those thoughts each time we conversed. I opened up to her only for her to go tell him every word I said. She got me so many times like this but I had no one else to talk to. I can honestly say that she has been the cause of alot of my pain, emotional and physical. She has been the cause of him beating me many times after she told him what I said.

Not to digress, I'm no psychologist but I would bet based on his behavior that he could be classified as a narcissistic/sadistic psychopath,if those disorders could be grouped together. I mean he committed atrocious acts against me and flipped them to blame me for his transgressions. So anyway he pulled into a parking lot and parked. He continued yelling at me and started stripping me of my gold jewelry. My youngest brother was in the backseat quiet. But every now and then he would ask him if he agreed with what he was saying. Of course my brother said that he did. This was another method he used to cause division within the family. He had a way of making each individual family member not trust the other. He had each of us individually believing that one didn't like or care for the other. I can say that we all were pawns in his deranged game of chess. In retrospect I cannot believe that I lived in such a dysfunctional family. His method of controlling us is reminiscent of some cult leader. He desired to be the nucleus of the family,like he was a god. He used manipulative tactics to acquire this fear and worship.

My mind was racing as I sat in the front passenger seat. I was thinking myself up on what I had planned to do. I had to psych myself out. So I thought to myself, what good am I? What can I offer my children? I have no control in my life anyway! I'm good for nothing! My children won't miss me that much. They'll get over it, they're strong. So I pulled out the bottle of Xanax from my pocket. He saw the bottle and asked me what I was doing. I told him that I was tired of this, I was tired of everything. He then said "I don't give a fuck, kill yourself". I then got out of the car crying. I opened the bottle and dumped them all into my mouth and chewed them. I realize now that I was out of my mind but who could blame me.

Anyone who's ever tasted Xanax knows that it is one of the most bitter tasting pills. And yet I chewed them all, completely ignoring the awful taste.

After chewing them there was a small ball of Xanax in my mouth. I was about to swallow this ball but then a voice within said that my children need me. How can I just leave them in his care. At least they have a fighting chance with me here. I then decided to spit the ball out. I started walking up the street and my legs became heavy. He pulled up beside me and ordered me to get into the car. I got in and he started yelling at me. "Why would you do something so stupid". "Kill yourself because of money, you are so weak".

By this time I was in and out of consciousness. I recall being driven to the ER by him and that's it. I woke up what turned out to be over 24 hours later in a hospital bed with a Catheter inserted. Apparently I swallowed a good deal of the Xanax that had mixed with my saliva. Later that evening after I woke up, Greg came to visit me. Needless to say I wasn't happy to see him. He asked me how I was doing and I replied that I was doing fine. He didn't really care but there was a nurse sitting by my bed and he always had to put on a good face around strangers. So he asked me when I was going to be discharged. I told him that I didn't know. Honestly I wasn't in a rush to be discharged. He then told me to ask my R.N. I asked her and she said that she will find out for me. She came back in a short time later and said that once I spoke to the psychologist I could leave.

The psychologists came in a little while later and spoke to me in private. He asked me was I suicidal and I said no. He then said "Well when you came into the ER you were asked if you tried to kill yourself and you said yes". I told him that I wasn't thinking clearly and that "I don't want to die but want to go home to be with my children". He said "All right then" and exited the room. He wasn't the most pleasant person but I guess he gets tired of seeing suicidal people. After all he works in Atlantic City, the gambling capital of the East Coast. Greg then re-enters the room and says "So you're ready to go"? He told me to hurry up which I did. As we were leaving the hospital room, security started following us ,telling me that I couldn't leave. Greg told me to keep walking and to ignore them. We got outside to the SUV and by this time they had already alerted the A.C P.D.

The police got involved and told me that I couldn't leave. They said that it was against state law. I was told by the police that I had to go back in the hospital on my own or they would have to arrest me and take me back inside. And if it came to that they would give me a criminal charge and I would have two issues to deal with instead of just one. So I agreed and walked back into the hospital thinking that I'll be back out shortly. Wrong!

We got back into the hospital room and the nurse asked me to have a seat on the bed, which I did. The next thing I know, this gigantic black guy rushed into the room, push me down and placed all kinds of restraints on me. But before he had both of my hands restrained, I took the phone that was by my bed and started hitting him with all my might. He was so huge that this didn't faze him. I didn't have a chance of getting away. In my opinion the way he violently pushed me was uncalled for. But any who long story short, I was hauled off to the Atlantic County psychiatric ward located in the Alanticare Regional Hospital. When I arrived they made sure that I didn't have anything I could use to harm myself or anyone else. I was to be there for a maximum of 72 hours as allowed by New Jersey state law. I was paired in a room with this old, homeless white lady. Each night she slept fully clothed. Coat, hat, and gloves included. She barely talked and she had a habit of throwing used toilet tissue all over the room, when she urinated or defecated. This environment was even stranger than when I was locked up as a teen. Here I was around people who had mental illness. I made friends with almost everyone there. Each I asked of their story and they told me. I have changed their names.

My main friends were, Mila. A forty something middle-class white woman who was married to a black man. She tried to take her life because she found out that he was cheating. Jesse, a late twenty something year old white woman who was addicted to Flexeril and Percocet. A 17-year-old white girl, Karen, who was already addicted to Roxie's (street slang for OxyContin). She told me that she was hooked on Roxie's and I had no clue what that was until I asked her and she told me. Then there was Julia, an Afro-Dominican woman who barely spoke any English and was there for having a nervous breakdown. An upper middle class late forty something white woman who suffered from deep depression. Nothing brought her joy, I mean nothing. She couldn't even muster a smile or any other emotion for that matter. Her situation was so dire that her daughter signed to send her to Ancora (largest psychiatric hospital in South Jersey) to receive more shock therapy. I didn't know that was still in practice. This mid-30's black woman,Donna, who was pregnant with her fourth child. She suffered from paranoid schizophrenia. I felt the sorriest for her unborn baby who was being exposed to those harmful, experimental, mental medications. An Hispanic guy,Jorge', who was probably in his late 20's. He was out of it mostly because of the mental medications. When he first heard someone call my name he came to life. Saying loudly "Shakira, Shakira" like Wyclef Jean said in the song Hips don't lie by the Latina singer Shakira. There was another time when he walked up to me and put his hands in a praying position and asked "Shakira, can I please go home"? Taken back, I calmly responded with "Yes, you can go home". The next day I saw him being transported out of the ward. I'm not sure where to but it was rumored to be Ancora. And from what I was told by all of my friends no one wants to go to Ancora. It's rumored (by the people who have been there) to be the place where ill treatment was taken on a higher level. There were many more patients but these people I actually befriended.

While there I had to participate in all sorts of childish activities. I blocked out how the staff talked to me like a three-year-old. My aim was to get out of there ASAP. While there I started to think deeply about my situation. Why was I here? Did I really want to die? What would make me happy? Does my depression stem from my home environment? Isn't my mother's boyfriend/rapist/woman beater/baby's father the one with the problem? Why is he not here?

As I read a book on Native American spirituality the true answers to these questions became clear. In my heart I knew that I had to change. I realized that if I didn't get out he was going to kill me. If not physically, then most certainly spiritually. This was a great life lesson that I wouldn't trade. I was in the company of people who truly had problems, ones they couldn't control. Brain chemical imbalances or whatever the cause of mental illness is. These beautiful, kind, loving people had problems that they couldn't help. And here I was letting some monster drive me to the brinks of death. I often think of my friends I met while there and wonder how they're doing now.

So finally after three days I was discharged with a diagnosis of suicidal ideation and depression. I wasn't given any prescribed medication while there but referred to see a counselor in my area.

When I got out my mom, Greg and my two youngest children were there to pick me up. Greg wasn't happy to see me, he wasn't pleasant at all. It's funny because when he and my mother visited me and brought me food to eat, he would act nice. I guess he wanted to make sure that I kept my mouth shut. He immediately started accusing me of being drugged and raped. I explained to him that they were very professional and no form of physical contact was allowed. And that I wasn't given any medication, period. On the ride back home I tried not to let him get to me. I thought about my new outlook on life while in the hospital. I then focused on not just wanting better for my children and myself but actually working towards this reachable goal. I was so happy, elated to be back with my children. It didn't take long after before he not only accused me of being raped while at the hospital but started accusing me of cheating in the past. Now I am not a sexually promiscuous woman. And once I'm in a relationship, I will remain loyal to my partner. But even the phraseology he used showed how delusional he was. Correct me if I'm wrong but I thought a person could only cheat if they were in a consensual relationship with someone. My relationship with him was anything but consensual.

I became so sick and tired of his false allegations. I recall one day I was sitting on the bed and he was standing up. Yelling and cursing as usual. He said that I "Fucked around on him". After hearing him say this over and over again I got tired of hearing it. So I guess you can say I lost my mind for a moment. I yelled out as loud as I could "I don't want you, I never wanted you, you're holding me captive, you molester"! He had a belt in his hands that he was in the process of putting through his belt hoops. He fully removed it and started beating me with the buckle end of the belt. I was in so much pain. He got me a couple times on my legs but most of the hits were on my forearms as I tried to block the hits. He then made me recant what I said and I was forced to apologize for saying it. If there was something besides me he couldn't stand, it was to be told the truth about himself. You might as well cut him with a knife.

After years and years of these "cheating" accusations, I wanted to put it to rest. I was tired of him justifying hitting and degrading me in the name of vengeance. Vengeance for something I wasn't guilty of. So I suggested a lie detector test. Not because I wanted him as a companion or desired to prove my loyalty. I knew I was leaving, it was just a matter of how and when.

Firstly, I thought, prove my innocence and he'll stop hitting me etc. Secondly, I wanted to prove to my children, especially my sons, that their mother wasn't a whore. I knew that was essential for them to maintain their respect of me. My daughters and sister knew better. Sometimes boys think differently of their mother constantly hearing things like this. Particularly when they've been basically programmed after hearing this garbage for numerous years.

So Greg agreed but I couldn't call the polygrapher myself. My mom or sister had to call to schedule the appointment. After this was done, in about three weeks time, the money for the test was saved. The examiner that was chosen was a retired NYPD detective who was based in North Jersey. But he worked the tri-states of Connecticut, New York and New Jersey. He traveled to the location and did the polygraph in the individual's home. This man was very reputable. He was on Ricki Lake, Maury Povich and a few other talk shows I couldn't remember. The polygrapher came over to our apartment. But before he came in, my mom's boyfriend had this little discussion with me. "I'm so proud of you for taking this test. Even if you fail the test, we can work through it. I have mad respect for you. A lot of women wouldn't do what you're doing" he said. "I appreciate what you're saying but I'm going to pass this test" I replied. Greg even withheld all of my prescription medication for a week prior to the test. So that it wouldn't interfere with the results.

The examiner entered the apartment, introduced his self and we offered him a seat. He talked to us for about an hour. Explaining the whole process, how the results are obtained, his diplomacy etc. He then asked if Greg had the questions written down that he wanted asked. Greg provided him a line of questions and then the examiner asked that he excuse himself from the room, which he did.

The examiner strapped me up to all kinds of wires connected to his laptop that was installed with the necessary software. I don't recall exactly how long it took but he asked me 10 questions that were written by Greg and 10 questions that he himself asked me to gauge my heart rate, pulse etc. After he finished he called Greg back into the room, where he gave and went over the results of the test. I passed of course. That was no surprise to me. Greg had this disappointed look on his face. He started asking the man about accuracy and asked could the system be tricked? The polygrapher explain as he had earlier that the best of criminals couldn't trick the system. Especially without the use of drugs. And even then he could tell if they were under the influence by their heart rate and pulse. He'd then reiterated its accuracy rate. He talked with us a little while longer to make sure that we were clear. Greg offered to walk him to his car, which the man accepted. My mom's boyfriend came back into the apartment telling me that the polygrapher told him something different. He claimed that the man told him that I failed the test. I then said "I don't believe you, let me call him". Why would he lie like that? Greg then said "No don't call him, you can call him but not today".

I was so happy to report the results to everyone. I told my daughter, sister, mom and sons. Greg had this dumb look on his face. He did however muster a very insincere smile. As I've explained numerous times, you're probably tired of me repeating it but here goes. I could NOT win for losing. He could ask me to jump and I ask how high and would conquer the task. He would say something like the landing wasn't smooth enough. Now this scenario didn't actually happen. I'm only attempting to give you a better understanding. This example may not be the best but hopefully you get the picture.

His violent nature wouldn't ease. Even though he found out that I hadn't been intimate with anyone on any level. My being banished to the children's room became ever so frequent. Which made me very happy, him being the devil he is, sensed this. So he would come into the room and forbid anyone to turn the TV on. Then it was the air conditioner if it were hot outside. We would all talk amongst each other or read books. Whenever he heard us laughing, he would do whatever necessary to stop it. From coming into the room hurling insults at everyone to throwing water, juice, condiments or whatever to shutting off all power to the room. I recall once when he sent me into the room, not 10 minutes later, he started threatening to kill us, all of us. I was shocked and horrified. We shut the door and he tried to push it open. So my sons pushed a drawer chest in front of the door so that we could barricade ourselves in the room. Next he came to the door, yelling for me to open the door. When no one did he started piercing the door with a chef knife. Those doors were made of very thin wood veneer so the knife went through it like nothing. Around that time a Pennsauken, NJ man had just killed his two sons, attempted to kill his third and then killed himself. Knowing of this I didn't think that it couldn't happen to us. So out of pure fear, I sent my oldest son out the bedroom window to call the police. When he heard my son exiting through the window he left for the front door and tried to chase my son. Yelling how he was going to "Kill that nigga". My son managed to outrun him. Not long after my son left the apartment, Greg sent my mother to the door to convince me not to tell what happened. My daughter and sister moved to drawer chest. I then went into the front room when the police were outside. My mother told me to say that my brother and I got into an argument and that he threatened to get a knife.

Not knowing the next move to make, not having any money or valuables, not having anywhere to go, I did as my so-called mother asked. When the police questioned me they were very polite and patient. I was close to tears when one of the officers stated that my son was talking delusional. He hinted that my son could be using drugs. In retrospect, I now know where the officer got this notion. It turns out that this particular officer had spoken to Greg first. I believe that Greg gave the police officer this idea. I know for a fact that my son wasn't using drugs or hadn't used drugs. I know for a fact that his "Grandfather" (as told by Greg to the police) was indeed my sons' biological father. I know for a fact that he alone stabbed through the bedroom door just minutes earlier. But I had to stand there and fight back tears. I don't blame the police they had not a clue of the hell we were going through and I at that point was too afraid to tell them.

I think Greg always feared his sons to a certain degree. He sought to break them down so that they would never be tempted to stand up to him in my defense. I myself felt so humiliated by him, that I cut myself twice with a pocket knife on two different occasions. Feeling this pain helped take my mind from the frustration and powerlessness I felt. I thank God that it didn't become an addiction as I've read some people develop.

After not telling what actually happened the night when he threatened to kill us. He still degraded me. He still hit me. He still tortured me. Because of an pending trial, I won't discuss what led to his current incarceration. What I will say is that one night as I lie in bed questioning God, I was honestly about to give up on God. I couldn't understand why would God allow these things to happen to me. I saw how real God is. How God is all powerful but he wouldn't put away this mortal demon. Why God? Why? I never did anything to hurt anyone. Though not perfect I have a pure heart. I had been the victim for so many years at that point. I then had an epiphany. How can I say that I have faith when I haven't lost fear. If I make one step, then God will help me make two. At that moment I truly lost fear. A number of things were done to me that led to his current charges. But once I went to the police he was held in their custody on several serious felonies.

After I got back home from the police station ,I knew that I had to make my break. Three weeks before I went to police, he had brought a new flatscreen TV, a PlayStation gaming console, additional controls and multiple games. I had the receipts in my pocketbook. I told my children to package those things. I had to take them back to the store. There was no other money. After I returned everything I had about $1500 cash. My children and I got all of our clothes and necessities that could fit into the Durango (He sold the Escalade and got a smaller SUV). I asked my mother to drive us to the train station. She had already driven us to each store to return the items. She agreed and surprisingly didn't try hard to convince us to stay. There was nothing she could say that would have changed my mind anyway. From the train station we took a cab to a motel far away. I was 32 years old when I finally escaped. I had never truly had my own apartment, nor did I have my license much less know how to drive and I didn't have my high school diploma. This is not the end of my story. I have so much more to share with you. I wrote this book manually in red ink. I chose red ink because symbolically, I was bleeding. Bleeding unto the paper. What I have shared with you was not easy my friends. No, I am not a scholar nor am I a renowned author. And maybe I haven't used the fanciest of words but what I speak to you is verily true. I have shared with you my most painful afflictions. If my pain may enlighten and help others who are victims of rape,child molestation, domestic violence or any kind of sexual or nonsexual exploitation have a voice, so be it. Together my friends we can put an end to this madness that happens each day around the globe behind closed doors. Thank you all for allowing me to give.

I Have included some of my poetry that was written in the time of my captivity.Poetry was the only outlet I had that seemed to help keep me together. It was my only sanctuary.I had never planned to publish these or allow anyone to read them. Some of my poetry was destroyed by my captor/abuser.These are what I've managed to keep from being destroyed.I also have included the dates on which these poems were written. I am not a trained poet. Nor do I follow the rules of the many forms of poetry. I guess you can say though that I'm more of a free verse style poet. All this being said,I sincerely hope that you enjoy these very intimate poems just the same.

COLLECTIVE REFLECTIVE POEMS:

Photo taken by Shakira Z.Chi

"MR.MANIPULATION"
WRITTEN ON JUNE 28,2003

WHAT IS THE SOLUTION TO THIS MISERY THAT HE INFLICTS ON ME? HIS NAGGING,JUDGMENTAL,SELFISH,CALLOUS HEART. HOW DO I STAY STRONG,PRESS ON WITHOUT ABSORBING HIS DEMEANING WORDS? HIS EYES,HIS FISTS,HIS WORDS ALL CUT LIKE A SWORD. I HAVE SO MUCH TO SHARE,A BREATH OF LIFE TO BREATHE BUT MR.MANIPULATION WON'T LET ME BE. AS I LOOK INTO THE MIRROR I DON'T SEE ANY HOPE. WILL I FOREVER BE ON THE SHORT END OF MR.MANIPULATION'S ROPE? MY SOUL IS SHATTERED-I FEEL I HAVE NO WORTH. MR.MANIPULATION IS TO BLAME,HE'S THE BEGINNING OF ALL THIS PAIN.

Photo taken by Shakira Z.Chi

"UNJUST RULER"
WRITTEN ON JUNE 21,2006

UNJUST RULER, MY PRECEPTS YOU MISCONSTRUE. CONDEMN ME, BURDEN ME, NEVER UNDERSTAND ME, HOLD MY HONOR TO BE YOUR FRIEND. QUIETLY APPROACHING MY WITS END.YOUR GOAL IS TO APPREHEND MY SOUL. THROW OFF KEY MY INTELLECTUAL AND EMOTIONAL DISPOSITION. OVERTHROW MY JOY YOUR ONLY MISSION. WHEN I AM FREE,WHEN I AM FREE. UNJUST RULER'S GOAL IS TO RAZE MY INNER QUALITIES. UNJUST RULER DAMNED BE YOUR ESTATE,THOUGH THIS PATH I HAD TO TAKE SO THAT I MAY ONE DAY RECOGNIZE TRUE GOODNESS AND A TRANQUIL STATE.

photo taken by Shakira Z.Chi

"INNER INSIGHT"
WRITTEN ON FEBRUARY 23,2007

ANGER IS THE WORST FORM OF SUFFERING- HOSTILITY LINGERING.COMPARABLE TO A NUCLEAR BOMB CONSUMING OUR OXYGEN. CONTEMPT,A BATTLE THAT'S DIFFICULT TO WIN. FREE MYSELF FROM EVIL ENERGY THEN MAYBE I CAN LEARN TO LOVE AGAIN. HATE I MUST FIGHT,SMILING LIKE THE DAY BUT INSIDE I FEEL LIKE ITS NIGHT. I'M COLD AND ALONE, I'M ON MY OWN. ASPIRATIONS THAT ARE DISMANTLED THANKS TO THE EVIL ONE WITH MUCH DELIGHT. HAVING ALREADY DEALT WITH SOME OF THE MOST CRUEL METHODS OF TORTURE. I PRAY THAT ONE DAY GOD GIVES ME THE ABILITY TO FORGIVE MY ENEMY FOR ALL THE PAIN HE HAS IMPOSED ON ME. SO THAT MY SOUL MAY REST IN PEACE. I WILL NOT BE IN TURMOIL ANYMORE. WITH ALL MY HEART,GOD THIS IS WHAT I'M ASKING FOR. ANGER PLEASE TAKE IT AWAY FROM ME AT HEAVENS DOOR.

photo of Shakira Z. Chi

"THE FIGHT"
WRITTEN ON MARCH 13, 2009

DAY AND NIGHT A FIGHT THAT'S SPIRITUAL. SUNSHINE TIMES WHEN HAPPY, UPRIGHT NOT UPTIGHT. BY A BLINK NIGHT FALLS AND HAPPINESS THAT WAS POSSESSED HAS LEFT. VENGEANCE IN MY MIND-HATE IN MY HEART-FOR THAT MOMENT JUST THAT MOMENT-DAY-HORUS, RA, CREATOR OF ALL. MY DAYS WILL LAST THIS LIFETIME AND BEYOND. NIGHT- SET, HATE, DESTRUCTIVE ENERGIES WILL NOT WIN. ALTHOUGH EACH DAY I EXPERIENCE THIS AGAIN AND AGAIN. MY CYCLE OF LIFE. ANGER, DESPAIR WE ALL HAVE BUT SOME ARE UNAWARE. REMOVE ONESELF FROM DARK ENERGIES AND YOU WILL FIND THAT YOU'LL BE SHROUD BY DAYLIGHT, SUNSHINE ,HAPPINESS. NEVER LET NIGHT GET THE BEST OF US. SET BE CAST INTO DARKNESS WHERE YOU WILL FOREVER DWELL. DAY NIGHT A CONSTANT FIGHT. ON MY QUEST TO UNDO A WICKED SPELL.

HYPOCRITES
WRITTEN ON AUGUST 20,2009

SOME BEINGS WHO SAY THEY DON'T BUT IN ACTUALITY THEY DO,SHAKING THEIR VERBAL STICKS AT YOU; ATTEMPTING TO KEEP YOU IN LINE. MATTER OF FACT ALL OF THEIR WORDS ARE AN EXUBERANCE OF LIES,IN DISGUISE AS A SAINT TO THIS WORLD,BUT HE IS A DEVIL IN MY EYES. BE NOT WISE IN YOUR OWN EYES,HYPOCRITE!!

photo taken by Shakira Z. Chi

"PUSH FORWARD"
WRITTEN ON SEPTEMBER 11,2009

PUSH FORWARD IN WHATEVER YOU DO. YOUR HAPPINESS IS UP TO YOU. IN LIFE PEOPLE WILL ATTEMPT TO BREAK YOU DOWN. FRIENDS WHO YOU THOUGHT WERE ARE NOT AROUND. ALL OF THE GLEE THAT WAS ONCE SHOWN SHORTLY BECOMES AN FROWN. BUT YOU MUST PUSH FORWARD; FAITH WOULD BE WORD ANOTHER FOR IT. OBSTACLES JUST ANOTHER CHAPTER IN THIS BOOK OF LIFE. FOR AS LONG AS WE'RE ALIVE THERE WILL BE STRIFE. DON'T LET ANOTHER'S VIEWS DOMINATE YOUR CROWN. PUSH FORWARD, KNOCK THOSE EMOTIONAL BARRIERS DOWN. I WILL PUSH FORWARD ON THOSE WHO TRY TO ROB MY ENERGY OF POSITIVITY. WHETHER THERE'S AN STORM,SNOW OR EXCESSIVE HEAT. PUSH FORWARD TO BE GOOD,DO NOT ACCEPT DEFEAT! PUSH FORWARD IS WHAT MY CREATOR HAS REVEALED TO ME THIS DAY. TO PUSH FORWARD IS THE ONLY WAY.

Photo of Queen Puabi's costume ,taken by Shakira Z. Chi

"HATE OF HATE"
WRITTEN ON NOVEMBER 11,2009

A HATE SO OLD AND DEEP THAT IT BECOMES THE REASON FOR LOSS OF SLEEP. CONTEMPT SO HIDDEN THAT WHEN REVEALED YOU YOURSELF CAN NOT COMPREHEND IT. SO YOU DAY BY DAY AND NIGHT BY NIGHT TRANCE YOURSELF TO BELIEVE THAT EVERYTHING IS ALRIGHT. ENERGY ONE WITH UNIVERSE, CREATOR OF UNIVERSE ,CAUSING HARMFUL ENERGIES TO ONES WHO HAVE CAUSED YOU HARM. NOT ALARMED WHEN HIS CYCLE COMES FULL CIRCLE. FOR THAT I AM PREPARED. FOR ALL HIS TRANSGRESSIONS THE HEAVENLY FATHER IS AWARE. THE DIVINE ORDER FOR THOSE WICKED WILL COME TO PASS. KEEP MY SANITY? HARDLY,COVERING MY ANGUISH WITH VANITY. A QUICK FIX THAT BARELY DOES THE TRICK. OH GOD HEAR ME ,DELIVER ME FROM THIS HATE SO OLD AND DEEP,BEFORE HIS EVILNESS BECOMES A PART OF ME! ALL OF HIS CARDS HAVE BEEN DEALT. I AM HATE OF HATE. EVERY MOVE THAT WAS MADE INTENDED TO PLACE ME IN CHECKMATE. WHAT'S BEEN DONE TO ME IN MY BOOK HE CAN NEVER RECTIFY OR ERADICATE FOR I AM HATE OF HATE.

Photo taken by Shakira Z. Chi

"SATAN"(A NAME I THOUGHT FIT MY ABUSER)
WRITTEN ON MARCH 24,2010

SATAN PATHOLOGICAL LIAR , SELFISH , WARMONGER , TORTUROUS ,MATERIALISTIC NARROW MINDED,SADISTIC ,PREJUDICE, INSECURE, INFERIOR YEARNING TO BE SUPERIOR . THESE DESCRIPTIONS ARE ALL TOO FEW, SO WHEN YOU ACT LIKE YOU DON'T HAVE A CLUE. LOOK INTO THE MIRROR AND REALIZE THAT SATAN IS YOU!!

Photo taken by Shakira Z. Chi

"MIND SET"
WRITTEN ON JULY 11, 2010

I DO CONFESS THAT I WAS ENSNARED BY YOUR IDEOLOGIES , CAPTIVATED BY YOUR CHARMS. NOT ENLIGHTENED, TOO YOUNG TO SEE THAT CARING FOR YOU WOULD CAUSE ME GREAT HARM. BREAKING ME IS IN YOUR WILL,BUT BREAK ME YOU WON'T. CONFORM ME TO YOUR BELIEFS THINK SO, I DON'T. I AM A PRODUCT OF WHAT THE MOST HIGH WILLED ME TO BE. DESPISE ME BECAUSE I DON'T BLINDLY FOLLOW YOUR PHILOSOPHIES. WHAT DO YOU THINK YOU MEAN TO ME ? INDEED YOU HAVE OFFERED ME SEED OF THOUGHT. BUT I DETERMINE WHETHER THEY SPROUT AND GROW. I SEE YOU NOW IN THE LIGHT. MY SYNOPSIS - YOU'RE SPIRITUALLY VOID OF LIGHT. IN DARKNESS YOU DWELL , BY CHOICE OR BY FORCE UNABLE TO TELL. I MUST MOVE ON FOR YOU ARE ONLY A CHAPTER IN THIS BOOK OF LIFE. A GRUELING READ OF YESTERYEAR .OF TURNING THE PAGE I MUST LOSE FEAR!

Photo taken by Shakira Z. Chi

"TO WHOM IT MAY CONCERN"
WRITTEN ON SEPTEMBER 22,2010

THOSE WHO SO ELOQUENTLY CALL ME DUMB, POINTING THEIR FINGER CONSTANTLY,TELLS WHO THEY REALLY ARE. THOUGH I HAVE CARED FOR YOU, I'VE BEEN LEFT WITH DEEP EMOTIONAL SCARS. YOU ARE IN FACT DUMB. INFERIOR COMPLEX THE NEXUS OF YOUR SOUL AND MENTALITY.I'VE NEVER RAPED OR ABUSED. REALIZING,RATIONALIZING THAT I AM BETTER THAN THEE! TO WHOM IT MAY CONCERN; UNDERNEATH THIS CLOAK OF HATE SOMEWHERE LIES

LOVES. BRUISED, CONFUSED AND SUFFERING. INNOCENCE TAKEN AWAY BY THOSE WHO WERE TO PROTECT. OPTIMISM STRIPPED BY THOSE WHO NEGLECT.INTELLIGENT,CARING, SINCERE. I AM WHO I'VE ALWAYS BEEN. SO WHY THEN DO YOU PIERCE MY HEART AND RIP INTO MY SOUL? SCALD MY CHARACTER AND PROFESS TO BE MY FRIEND. TO WHOM IT MAY CONCERN,LIFE AS I DESIRE WILL SHORTLY BEGIN. YOU ARE NOT BLOOD OF MY BLOOD. TO THOSE WHO ATTEMPT TO BREAK ME DOWN TO MOLECULES,ATOMS AND NEURONS,HAVING NO MATTER. HEAR THIS THE CREATOR RULES NOT YOU! YOUR EVILNESS THE BANE OF MY EXISTENCE . STAGNATING YOUR CONTROL MY UTMOST GOAL. SO THAT I MAY ALWAYS MAINTAIN MY SOUL.

Photo taken by Shakira Z. Chi